Law Essentials

JURISPRUDENCE

Law Essentials

JURISPRUDENCE

Duncan Spiers, M.A. (Oxon)

Advocate;
Lecturer in Law, Edinburgh Napier University

DUNDEE UNIVERSITY PRESS
2011

Published in Great Britain in 2011 by
Dundee University Press
University of Dundee
Dundee DD1 4HN

www.dundee.ac.uk/dup

ISBN 978–1–84586–109–4

No natural forests were destroyed to make this product;
only farmed timber was used and replanted

British Library Cataloguing-in-Publication data
A catalogue for this book is available on request from the British Library.

Typeset by Waverley Typesetters, Warham
Printed and bound by Short Run Press Limited, Exeter

CONTENTS

TABLE OF CASES

TABLE OF STATUTES

1 INTRODUCTION

Jurisprudence as a subject ranges across a wide range of philosophical and sociological approaches to law. Students traditionally find the subject difficult as philosophical and sociological methods are different from those of "black-letter" law subjects. There are few cases to be encountered and one of them, Fuller's case of the Speluncian Explorers, is utterly fictitious. The questions posed are equally confusing. They too are very general and often seem to have little point. One question may generate a range of answers some of which are obvious and others cryptic. There is no correct answer. Students find it hard to draw a balanced view. Even worse, texts may be written in an obscure manner, using technical expressions. But it doesn't have to be this way. There are strong central themes.

This volume progresses through the main ideas of jurisprudence much in the order in which the subject may be encountered by students on an average law course. The writer has endeavoured to extract from the different positions the main arguments which lie at their heart. Exposed in this way, the major implications of the ideas should be reasonably clear.

Chapter 2 looks at Natural Law theory which starts with the assumption that laws should conform to moral standards aimed at forcing us to act ethically and thereby to develop a morally good character which is part of our human nature. A general overview of moral theories is discussed in Chapter 3 which concludes with Sir Neil MacCormick's ideas on practical reasoning. Chapter 4 examines Legal Positivism from its inception in Bentham's and Austin's Command Theory. We look at two influential modern forms, those of Kelsen and Hart. We also look at MacCormick's views on the institutions of law, sovereignty and judicial reasoning. Chapter 5 looks at Legal Realism which continues the theme of judicial decision-making but introduces social and psychological factors. Chapter 6 looks at historical, Marxist, anthropological and sociological theories. Chapter 7 gives an overview of power theories, Critical Legal Studies, Postmodernism and Feminism. The last three chapters, Chapters 8–10, examine three important concepts: rights, justice and punishment.

While the subject involves a wide range of methods from philosophy, criminology, sociology to psychology, the subject is capable of some unified explanation. Human beings have evolved to co-operate with each other in order to survive in hostile natural and social environments. As a species we have evolved forms of social behaviour to give us and our own social group the best chances of protection, survival and reproduction. Law is a social institution built upon our innate social behaviour and habits. Legal institutions provide the society which they regulate with a uniform set of understandings and of behavioural norms. Law provides mechanisms for achieving our purposes and meeting our needs without unnecessary hostility. It can be said that the more one questions law, the more our own human nature is reflected back at us. Our human nature is not perfect. We are driven by conflicting motives which need to be controlled if we are to live among our neighbours. Law can provide that element of control which forces us to consider our social obligations and live in peace. But in addition law can guide our practical day-to-day choices and lead us to live lives justly and virtuously. Even where laws are made and imposed by oppressive, greedy or megalomaniac rulers, or where laws are routinely broken by criminals, law may in the end be able to provide a form of justice. Law protects our strongly held values and defends us against the more predictable threats that may arise from our neighbours. These aspects of law are all reflected in the Schools of jurisprudential thought referred to above. For example, Legal Positivism and Realism see law principally as state power structures of one sort or another. Historical, anthropological and sociological theories concentrate on our natural social structures and institutions. Natural Law theories seek to improve the individual by guiding him morally and so to produce the higher ethical nature which is innate in us all.

While reading through the book, there are some aspects of every theory which need to be considered and which may act as keys to understanding. H L A Hart, in the Preface to *The Concept of Law*, wrote that his aim was "to further the understanding of law, coercion and morality as separate but related social phenomena". In doing so, Hart provides us with a ready list of aspects we should always keep in mind: (1) laws are systems of interrelated rules with all that that implies; (2) laws frequently make use of forms of coercion usually imposed by states; (3) laws may involve natural moral concepts; and (4) law is ultimately a social phenomenon which builds upon our innate forms of social organisation. These four aspects will guide and inform the student. Hart uses them to build a very powerful and controversial theory of law. He provides a means of drawing together the disparate jurisprudential questions and giving them a context previously hidden. His book is very important and has spawned a vast literature. Despite the occasional flaws in his argument, his insight remains durable, invaluable and authoritative. Getting to grips with Hart's concept is obviously an important goal for any student of jurisprudence. For many modern thinkers, jurisprudence is little more than footnotes on Hartian themes, and some courses in jurisprudence concentrate on Hart to the exclusion of much of importance that has been written since the publication of *The Concept of Law*. Space has prevented this fascinating journey into modern responses from being pursued within this book. For students it is important to get to grips with the foundations before building upon them. Nevertheless the author has made various references throughout the book to MacCormick's distinctive Scottish contributions in this area which, it is hoped, the student will find stimulating to further study.

2 NATURAL LAW

Natural Law theories assert that, while law is a human construct, there are higher moral principles which are accessible to us through our faculty of reason and which we may use to inform and give direction to our lives, to do justice and to judge the moral quality of laws. Using this higher law we can judge whether a law or an action is "right" or "wrong". We should avoid doing actions which are morally wrong. To help us we should be guided by laws that are morally right. Our faculty of reason will always guide us.

Laws are usually good. But we all criticise laws from time to time. We express our approval or disapproval of particular laws and government policies. We do this in different ways. We may grumble about some law or other; we may protest against a law; some may feel justified in taking more direct action; and, if an entire regime is judged to be evil, we may rise up and overthrow it.

When we ask what these higher values are, we find this harder to state. Natural Law theories rarely tell us what these values are. But our belief in higher values (or a "higher law") is frequently asserted. The higher law will always be a moral standard of some sort but sometimes it has a religious context.

Natural Law theories are roughly divided into classical or modern Natural Law theories. We shall look at each in turn and we shall see a number of very different approaches. A recurring theme is that the higher law in some way is recognised within us or is reflected in our social human nature and in particular our rational character. Despite the nebulousness of the idea of a higher law, we owe a continuing debt to Natural Law theories. This is because they require us to consider how far our human nature, especially our social nature, constrains the purposes for which law should be used. They also give rise to and provide a continuing justification for some important legal concepts which we now uncritically regard as being a necessary part of the law. Justice and the Rule of Law are examples. Arguably, human rights derive from Natural Law theories. Reaction to Natural Law has produced some important political concepts such as the Social Contract, the Rule of Law and possibly even the idea of democracy.

CLASSICAL NATURAL LAW

The origins of Natural Law are to be found in the ethical thinking of the Ancient Greeks and in particular of the Stoics, Plato and Aristotle. These thinkers held that natural things, including our human nature, are created with a natural tendency or movement towards the ends for which they have been created. Such a belief arose out of experience of things in the world. If you plant an acorn it will naturally grow into an oak tree. It will not develop into another kind of plant. The ability to develop into a tree of its own type is a feature which every type of seed has. The ends or goals to which things are innately directed are known by the Greek word *telos* and the idea of innate directedness in things is known as *teleology*. Human beings are part of the same world and, like everything else, we are directed towards the natural ends that are laid out for us and that lie in our human nature. For example, human beings naturally form relationships, procreate and bring up children in families. Such behaviour is natural to us. It is in this sense that Natural Law theories are described as "natural". They reflect our nature.

If we are to live at peace within our society and in harmony with our neighbours then we must learn to live ethically. Morality is at the heart of Natural Law. It is natural for us to form social bonds and live in harmony with the universe in this way. The Natural Law guides us in making good choices and acting rightly. Our nature is a mixture of animal and rational: we have contrary drives. Living ethically involves striking an appropriate balance between these alternating natural forces. Aristotle tells us that the ethical man or woman learns to live by moderation and to seek virtue. Living continuously by moderation and virtue enables a man or woman to develop a virtuous character. Only by so doing can a person find true happiness and fulfilment. Living in a manner which contradicts virtue contradicts also our human nature and ultimately brings only unhappiness. Ethical living therefore means learning to live in accordance with the nature which directs and makes meaningful our humanity. The Natural Law has an important part to play in this.

Roman Natural Law: Cicero

The Romans were the inheritors of these Greek ideas. No educated Roman could ignore Greek ethics. But while the Greeks were not great lawyers, the Romans were. It is therefore in Roman legal writing that we find the first clear formulation of a Natural Law. Cicero set out to explain the fact that the laws of the Romans and those of neighbouring states tended to coincide in essentials. He suggested that they did so necessarily because all such laws were in accordance with our human nature. He said (in *De Re Publica; De legibus*):

> "true law is right reason in agreement with nature; it is of universal application, unchanging and everlasting; its summons us to duty by its commands and averts from wrongdoing by its prohibitions. And it does not lay its commands or prohibitions upon good men in vain, though neither have any effect on the wicked. It is a sin to try to alter this law, nor is it allowable to attempt to repeal any part of it, and it is impossible to abolish it entirely. We cannot be freed from its obligations by Senate or people, and we need not look outside ourselves for an expounder or interpreter of it. And there will not be different laws at Rome and Athens, or different laws now and in the future, but one eternal and unchangeable law will be valid for all nations and at all times, and there will be one master and ruler, that is, God, over us all, for he is the author of this law, its promulgator, and its enforcing judge. Whoever is disobedient is fleeing from himself and denying his human nature, and by reason of this very fact he will suffer the worst penalties, even if he escapes what is commonly considered punishment".

It is a common mistake to interpret a passage like this as indicating that values come from religion. This error is even easier to make when we examine Aquinas (below). The proper interpretation of Cicero's passage is that it is an ethical explanation of the laws and legal systems. We are guided by our nature just as is the rest of humankind. We are in a greatly privileged position over animals as we have the rational faculty to reveal moral values to us. Human beings, unlike animals, are aware that they have a nature and a purpose which the law is designed to fulfil. Law, unless it is corrupt, will embody the Natural Law. To live ethically in accordance with the Natural Law is easy as we have only to reflect and then we shall recognise what is the ethical course of action. That will always be in accordance with our human nature. It is for this reason that Cicero opens with the definition of law as "right reason in agreement with nature". Since we share our nature with all human beings, we should expect them to behave in similar ways and form similar moral judgments. The uniformity of law to which Cicero refers proves this point. If we share our natures, we should expect basic laws to be the same wherever in the world we look and whenever we look. This uniform law is often referred to as the *ius gentium* (the law of nations).

Aquinas

St Thomas Aquinas was an 11th-century Dominican friar who wrote a highly influential philosophical and theological work, the *Summa*

Theologica, which summarised and expressed in a systematic form all the knowledge of the time. It is an enormously lengthy book but it is beautifully and logically written. Aquinas divides his text into about 500 fundamental questions. Each question is sub-divided into Articles which are then answered in a similar way. First, a number of Objections to the Article will be stated, then Aquinas gives an Answer to the Article by arguing and summarising the issues, and finally he completes his consideration of the Article by responding to each Objection in turn. Aquinas drew extensively on the philosophy of Aristotle and on his Ethics. Aquinas wanted to show how the Cosmos was a good thing – planned, created and controlled by a beneficent and omnipotent God. The Cosmos is the theatre of God's activity and purposes and its structures reflect the Divine Will. Mankind is part of the Cosmos and our nature is continuous with it. It follows that God's activity and purposes are worked out in human nature. The universal Eternal Law, which directs the Cosmos towards its ends, directs mankind also.

God's guidance of the Cosmos may be analysed into four types of laws:

- First, there is the Eternal Law in which God writes His design for creation into the Cosmos, upholds the universe in being, and directs things towards their appointed ends. Without this guiding support, the universe would cease to be. God's purposes are known only to Him and cannot be comprehended by us. Aquinas writes:

    "Now God, by His wisdom, is the Creator of all things in relation to which He stands as the artificer to the products of His art. He governs all the acts and movements that are to be found in each single creature. The Divine Wisdom, inasmuch as by it all things are created, has the character of art, exemplar or idea: moving all things to their due end, bearing the character of law. Accordingly the eternal law is nothing else than the type of Divine Wisdom, as directing all actions and movements." (*Summa,* Part II, Question 92, Article 1)

- Second, there is the Natural Law, whereby God imbues all things with purposes and a striving to fulfil those purposes. Men and women can see this force at work. The spider, for example, builds a web to catch its prey. It has no intellectual understanding of this but its natural behaviour, built into it by God, guides it to build a web which is both perfect for its purposes and in addition is an object of great beauty. We may reflect on this behaviour and thereby contemplate the power, majesty and beneficence of God. The natural world is full of similar such examples. Mankind, as part of nature, is also guided by internal forces and is thus guided by the Natural Law. This is nowhere more obvious than in our natural faculty of reason. The Natural Law is a general revelation of God's purposes revealed through our very nature. Aquinas writes:

> "We see that things which lack intelligence, such as natural bodies, act for an end, and this is evident from their acting always, or nearly always, in the same way, so as to obtain the best result. Hence it is plain that not fortuitously, but designedly, do they achieve their end. Now whatever lacks intelligence cannot move towards an end, unless it be directed by some being endowed with knowledge and intelligence ... this being we call God." (*Summa*, I, 2, 3)

- Third, there is the Divine Law. This part of God's law is required because we are created free and moral beings. We have been given the freedom to choose our actions. This means that it is possible for us to sin, to disobey God and to act contrary to our nature. Sin can cause us to follow destructive paths and behave self-interestedly. Ultimately, sin would lead us to destruction but God does not will this to be so. The scriptures therefore tell us of how God has intervened in history to reveal His particular purposes for mankind, to discipline and punish His people, the Israelites, and to reveal His general purposes for them and for all believers. The Ten Commandments are a specific and important source of the Divine Law revealed to mankind. They contain a sum of the most important moral and religious values which are revealed to us in order to make us fit to receive divine grace. The Divine law is therefore a particular revelation of God's purposes revealed in history.

- Fourth, there is the Human Law. This is the law which is created by earthly rulers. Properly construed, God has delegated some of His creative power to humankind who thus share with God in the creative power as partners in the creative work. Our role in the world is to be stewards of God's creation and to act creatively and morally. Such work should be conducted with solemnity and justice. This is a very positive view of the Cosmos and of mankind's part in it. Human laws therefore enable us to lead the virtuous life. Aquinas writes:

> "Man has a natural aptitude for virtue; but the perfection of virtue must be acquired by man by means of some kind of training. Thus we observe that man is helped by industry in his necessities, for instance, in food and clothing. Certain beginnings of these he has from nature, for example his reason and his hands; but he has not the full complement, as other animals have, to whom nature has given

sufficiency of clothing and food ... Therefore in order that man might have peace and virtue, it was necessary for laws to be framed." (*Summa*, II, 95, 1)

Our rulers perform their share in Divine creation by means of enacted law. Such laws are good and should be obeyed. Good laws have a binding power on subjects as they are an extension of God's rule mediated through human rulers. Aquinas writes:

"Now laws are said to be just ... when ... they are ordained to the common good: from their author, that is to say, when the law that is made does not exceed the power of the lawgiver; and from their form when burdens are laid on the subjects, according to an equality of proportion and with a view to the common good." (*Summa*, II, 96, 4)

Unfortunately human acts are not always righteous. Just as individual men and women can sin, so can rulers. In so doing, evil rulers exceed their authority and contradict the powers they have been given. They may become tyrants and act unjustly. It is therefore possible for a human law to diverge from the Divine Will. Where a human law diverges from the Natural Law in this way, it is a perversion of law. On reflection, we will see that such a law is a bad law. Bad laws have no binding power on subjects. While we must obey good laws, we have no obligation to obey bad laws. This does not mean that we must disobey bad laws. We are simply loosed from the bonds of duty in relation to them. In practice, such bad laws do not bind the conscience but we should nevertheless continue to obey them except where to do so would create a greater evil such as lawlessness, scandal or a great harm. In particular, a human law which opposes the Divine plan should never be obeyed. Aquinas writes:

"Laws may be unjust through being opposed to the Divine good: such are the laws of tyrants inducing to idolatry, or to anything else contrary to the Divine law: and laws of this kind must nowise be observed, because we ought to obey God rather than man ... This argument is [also] true of a law that inflicts unjust hurt on its subjects. The power that man holds from God does not extend to this: wherefore neither in such matters is man bound to obey the law, provided he avoid giving scandal or inflicting a more grievous hurt." (*Summa*, II, 96, 4)

It will be seen that Aquinas's version of Natural Law, though expressed in religious terms, remains true to the aims of all Natural Law thinking in that it provides mankind with the ability to lead a good and virtuous life. This is achieved through the guidance of moral principles and good laws.

Grotius

Hugo Grotius (1583–1645) used Natural Law principles to develop a theory of international law whereby nation states could live together peacefully. Grotius set out to discover universally applicable rational principles which he could universalise and apply as the answers to problems in international law. Grotius was a Dutch Protestant but he maintained that his Natural Law methods would be equally valid even if there had been no God. He formed the view that an action is good not because it was willed by God but, on the contrary, God would only will those acts which are morally good. In doing so Grotius was expressing the view that Natural Law could be logically independent of theological truths. This is a most important step in the development of Natural Law theory.

Grotius's work on *Just War* (*De Jure Belli ac Pacis*) remains a most important treatise in international law. He builds his theory upon ideas of natural justice, the obligation to act in self-defence, the entitlement of a harmed party to reparation, and punishment being imposed on those who have done harm. Here is a brief extract showing his method of reasoning:

> "The first inquiry ... is, whether any war be just, and, in the next place, what constitutes the justice of that war. For, in this place, right signifies nothing more than what is just, and that, more in a negative than a positive sense; so that RIGHT is that, which is not unjust. Now any thing is unjust, which is repugnant to the nature of society, established among rational creatures. Thus for instance, to deprive another of what belongs to him, merely for one's own advantage, is repugnant to the law of nature, as Cicero observes in the fifth Chapter of his third book of offices; and, by way of proof, he says that, if the practice were general, all society and intercourse among men must be overturned."

Hobbes and the Social Contract

Thomas Hobbes was not a Natural Lawyer. He rejected the idea that law should be guided by some form of justice revealed in our human nature. On the contrary, and probably as a result of living in a time of revolution, he had a very pessimistic view of human nature. Human nature, however, was the starting point of his theory of the Social Contract. Hobbes thought that in our natural state we are selfish, greedy for power, violent and anarchic. Every man is at war with every other. In *Leviathan* he famously describes mankind's natural state as "solitary, poore, nasty, brutish and short" (*Leviathan*, Chapter 13). But, at the same time, every person has a desire for peace and recognises that the only way to achieve this is if everyone were simultaneously to lay down their arms and curtail their aggressive desires. This would make people vulnerable to others and so they would not do this voluntarily. This could only be done if someone more powerful forces them to do it and agrees to defend them against any aggressor.

Peace and political stability can be achieved only by the creation of a sovereign (whether a person or group of people) who can use the power of law to defend citizens. Hobbes imagines a mythical time when, to achieve peace, people elect one of their number to be their sovereign. The people enter into a contract with their appointed sovereign, making over all of their separate powers to him so that he may use those powers to impose peace and order upon his kingdom by using the power of law and physical force. In this way the sovereign would provide peace, safety and protection for his subjects and preservation of their community interests. Hobbes believed that it was necessary to transfer to the sovereign *all* of our separate powers. His reason for this is that the sovereign must be master over all and subject to no-one. The all-powerful sovereign will use the powers in the form of laws and so bend our natural war-like and selfish inclinations to his will. Hobbes writes:

> "The only way to erect such a common power, as may be able to defend them from the invasion of forraigners, and the injuries of one another, and thereby to secure them in such sort, as that by their owne industrie, and by the fruites of the earth, they may nourish themselves and live contentedly; is to conferre all their power and strength upon one man, or assembly of men, that may reduce all their wills, by plurality of voices, unto one will … and in him consisteth the essence of the commonwealth; which to define it is one person, of whose acts a great multitude, by mutual covenants one with another, have made themselves everyone the author, to the end he may use the strength and means of them all, as he shall think expedient, for their peace and common defence. And he that carrieth this person is called Soveraigne, and said to have Soveraigne Power; and everyone besides, his subject." (*Leviathan*, Chapter 18)

One notable feature of Hobbes's form of the Social Contract is that all subjects are made equal, for none has any powers remaining. The idea of equality is therefore necessary to the idea of the Social Contract. The sovereign thus created holds all temporal power of the subjects and is subject to no other power except God. From such a sovereign would flow peace, honours and stability. A just sovereign would remain guided by God. Hobbes describes at great length the liberties and security which a just sovereign would bring. He describes the state thus created as a "commonwealth" and the actions of a just sovereign as "paternall" (which he contrasts with "despoticall"). Hobbes considered that a paternal sovereign appointed in this way would always act justly and he wrote at great length about the structures of the state and the undoubted benefits that would accrue to the Commonwealth. Hobbes did not appear to think that a properly appointed sovereign would act unjustly. He seems to think that the legal structures that such a sovereign would put into effect would serve to remove such a possibility. But Hobbes did grant that a ruler could be despotic and unjust. He believed that such a situation would be most unlikely and would come about only where there had been a conquest or victory in war by a "despot". In such circumstances, those under a despot's subjection would "have no obligation at all; but may break their bonds ... and kill, or carry away their Master, justly!" (*Leviathan*, Chapter 20).

David Hume

Hume was an Edinburgh philosopher of the 18th-century Enlightenment who set out to analyse human nature and thereby acquire true and certain knowledge. Hume believed that the only true knowledge of things was to be arrived at through the perceptions of the senses. In many ways Hume's idea of knowledge acquisition can be likened to a person sitting in a darkened room, viewing the world outside through a window. The person inside the room can only know of the external world by means of the impressions of things that they see through the window. In the same way Hume thinks that we can only know about the external world through the impressions of things communicated to us through our sense perceptions. For Hume, the whole process of learning about the world is essentially a passive one. It seems the mind has little if any work to do. Hume insists in philosophical scepticism. One should only acknowledge as true information that which is derived directly from the senses. About everything else, one had to be radically sceptical. Hume's method is often described as "empirical" since it is based on knowledge of facts acquired through observation, experience and experiment.

Hume's empirical method was a useful and timely method for the sciences but it had its limits. Some things did not seem to fit with his empirical method. In building up his philosophy, Hume relied upon the relation of cause and effect. He thought it was therefore essential to provide a proper foundation for this relation. Yet the relation could not be known through the empirical method. It was a supposition. All one could know about causation was that causes and effects were experienced as constant conjunctions of phenomena. The relation itself defied proof. Induction also defied proof by the empirical method. Induction is the name given for that method whereby it is possible to make generalities of explanation and infer future events from the constant and undeviating experience of the past. Hume realised that it was, of course, strictly impossible to acquire knowledge of the future behaviour of things. The sun may have risen every day in the past, but could one know – really know – that it will rise tomorrow morning? To deny such knowledge seems absurd, but as an item of knowledge, it cannot in principle be derived from empirical experience.

Nor could the empirical method explain mathematics, aesthetics, religion, law or morality. This caused Hume some concern. He concluded that the only thing that was real about law and morality was the fact that people customarily believed in principles of law and morality and so these legal and moral principles came to affect social behaviour. There was no other sense in which these subjects could give "true" knowledge.

In connection with morality, Hume famously held the view that an "ought" of morality could not be derived from an "is" of what is perceived by the senses. Just because human beings do form relationships, procreate and have children does not mean that they *ought* to do so. Hume writes:

> "In every system of morality, which I have hitherto met with, I have always remark'd. That the author proceeds for some time in the ordinary way of reasoning, and establishes the being of a God, or makes observations concerning human affairs; when of a sudden I am surpriz'd to find, that instead of the usual copulations of propositions, *is* and *is not*, I meet with no proposition that is not connected with an *ought*, or an *ought not*. The change is imperceptible; but is, however, of the last consequence. For as this *ought* or *ought not* expresses some new relation or affirmation, 'tis necessary that it shol'd be observ'd and explain'd; and at the same time that a reason should be given, for what seems altogether inconceivable, how this new relation can be a deduction from others, which are entirely different from it. But as authors do commonly use this precaution, I shall presume to recommend it to the readers; and am persuaded, that this small attention wol'd subvert all the vulgar systems of morality, and let us see, that the distinction of vice and virtue is not founded merely on the relations of objects nor is perceiv'd by reason."

This appears to be a knock-down argument for morality if Hume's empirical method is correct, and most people believed it was. It seemed that morality was a myth. With its loss classical Natural Law would have to draw to a close too. However, in the mid-20th century new forms of Natural Law survived this devastating attack.

MODERN NATURAL LAW THEORIES

Lon Fuller and the Inner Morality of Law

Fuller disagreed with a view that law and morality had to be kept separate. He saw a new and important way in which rationality entered the picture. He called this the "Inner Morality" of law. For rules of morality to be effective in guiding us, it seems to be necessary for certain procedural standards to be followed. Without these standards, rules simply cannot work at all. And if rules cannot work then there can be no principles of morality or law. It follows that the procedural standards are a necessary prerequisite of any morality and indeed of any law or other rule-ordered activity. But what are these procedural standards? To answer this question Fuller invents the allegory of King Rex. The allegory is found in Fuller's "The Morality of Law" at the beginning of Chapter 2.

King Rex came to the throne filled with zeal as a reformer, but he failed to make good laws because he did not know the eight procedural standards. He had to learn about them the hard way. He repealed all the old laws and produced a new code. But he had not been educated and the code was defective as he could not make even the simplest of generalisations. He decided to make amends for this by deciding cases himself. But his decisions were inconsistent and no pattern of decision-making could be discerned by anyone. He took lessons on generalisation and rewrote the code. But he kept it secret. People did not know what the code contained and so could not use it as a guide for action. Rex then decided he would decide all of a year's cases in the following year, giving a full explanation for his decisions. That would set out the legal principles people must follow for that year of the cases. Again, people objected as they were being expected to obey rules that would not be revealed to them until the following year. Rex produced a new code but it was so obscure that people could not understand it. Yet another code was prepared that was beautifully clear and precise but contained many contradictory rules. A new code was prepared which contained many new crimes, all to be given lengthy sentences. "It was made a crime, punishable by ten years' imprisonment, to cough, sneeze, hiccough, faint or fall down in the presence of the King." There were other provisions it was impossible to obey. Finally, a new code was prepared by experts: "The final result was, however, a triumph of draftsmanship. It was clear, consistent with itself, and demanded nothing of the subject that did not lie easily within his powers. It was printed and distributed free of charge on every street corner." However, the new code had taken so long to prepare that it was overtaken by events and it was necessary to put out amendments daily. If that were not bad enough, Rex resumed judging cases but his judgments bore no relation to the rules in the code.

By this means, Fuller asserts that the eight procedural standards, rationally required for any system of law, are:

(1) rules must first exist before people can use them for guidance and decision-making;

(2) rules must be publicised to the parties expected to obey them;

(3) rules must not be retroactive;

(4) rules must be understandable;

(5) rules should not contradict each other;

(6) rules must not require conduct beyond the ability of the affected party;

(7) changes must not be so frequent that people cannot orientate themselves to them; and

(8) there must be a congruence between rules as published and rules as administered.

A failure in any of these eight standards does not simply create a bad system of law – it fails to create any system of law at all. While Fuller calls these procedural standards an "Inner Morality", many have noted that it could just as easily produce a bad system of law as a good one. An effective evil regime would need to follow these procedures if it wished to promote its evil successfully. Some have shown that the Nazi regime, which had a very effective legal administration, adhered closely to these standards. There is therefore no guarantee that virtue would result from their use. Nevertheless, Fuller does provide a set of rational principles with enduring importance, of which all legislators should take notice, and which appears to avoid the "is"-to-"ought" shift. The standards are not the product of any empirical generalisation. They are necessary prerequisites for any rule-ordered activity.

John Finnis

Finnis also disagreed with the proposition that Natural Law attempts to derive an "ought" from an "is." He thought that it was still possible to grasp that one desires experiences which are a form of good for oneself and other humans. This conclusion would breach the "is"-to-"ought" shift if the goods one desired arose from an empirical analysis of human nature – and Natural Law theory is filled with those. Instead, if one could derive these goods from intuition alone, then that would suffice. Finnis says:

"From one's capacity to grasp intelligently the basic forms of good as 'to-be-pursued' one get's one's ability ... to see the point of actions, life-styles, characters, and cultures that one would not choose for oneself. And one's speculative knowledge of other people's interests and achievements does not leave unaffected one's practical understanding of the forms of good that lie open to one's choice. But there is no inference from fact to value, At this point our discourse (or private meditation), inference and proof are left behind (or left until later), and the proper form of discourse '... is a good, in itself, don't you think?'"

Finnis then sets out a list of seven "self-evident" basic goods (or 'basic forms of human flourishing') which include:

(1) life (corresponding to the drive for self-preservation) and possibly the transmission of life to children;

(2) knowledge considered as desirable for its own sake, and not merely instrumentally;

(3) play (engaging in activities enjoyed for their own sake);

(4) aesthetic experience (a response to beauty from outside one, and the "inner" appreciation and experience of beauty);

(5) sociability (friendship), ranging from peace and harmony among people to full friendship;

(6) practical reasonableness (being able to bring one's intelligence to bear effectively on the problems of choosing one's actions and lifestyle and shaping one's own character); and

(7) religion (the concern with "questions of cosmic order and of human freedom and reason").

He also sets out a list of interpretative "basic methodological require-ments" which are required in order for us to utilise the basic goods without distortion within our practical reasoning – that is to say that they are directed to how best to attain an appropriate balance of basic goods and promote the common good. We need not detain ourselves on the detail. Together these two lists make up the universal and unchanging principles of the Natural Law and show how we apply them in our practical moral choices.

Finnis's list of self-evident basic goods are said to provide for us all that is good for human individuals given the human nature that we share.

As with Aquinas, these goods have been derived not by understanding human nature from the outside (unlike Hume) but from the inside, as it were, by participation in and direct apperception of our human nature, by experiencing it from the inside in the form of one's desires, inclinations and motivations. Finnis asserts that there is no process of inference in this. One simply grasps that the basic good is a general form of good for oneself and others. While Finnis is concerned with practical morality, there is a connection with law. Law, in the Natural Law tradition, is there to guide us and show us the moral principles which will enable us to lead a good life, make good choices and seek after virtue. It follows that the law should respect and promote these basic forms of human flourishing ("basic goods"), since these will achieve those virtuous ends for individuals, and in addition attain the common good.

Essential concepts

- Natural Law theories assert that, while law is a human construct, there are higher moral principles which are accessible to us through our faculty of reason and which we may use to inform and give direction to our lives, to do justice and to judge the moral quality of laws. Our faculty of reason will always guide us.

- The origins of Natural Law are to be found in the ethical thinking of the Ancient Greeks and in particular of the Stoics, Plato and Aristotle. These thinkers held that natural things, including our human nature, are created with a natural tendency or movement towards the ends for which they have been created.

- If we are to live at peace within our society and in harmony with our neighbours then we must learn to live ethically. The Natural Law guides us in making good choices and acting rightly. Our nature is a mixture of animal and rational, we have contrary drives. Living ethically involves striking an appropriate balance between these alternating natural forces.

- Aristotle tells us that the ethical man or woman must live by moderation and seek virtue. Living by virtue enables a man or woman to develop a virtuous character. Only by so doing can a person find true happiness and fulfilment. Living in a manner which contradicts virtue contradicts also our human nature and ultimately brings only unhappiness.

- Cicero set out to explain the fact that the laws of the Romans and those of neighbouring states tended to coincide in essentials. He suggested they did so necessarily because all such laws were in accordance with our human nature. He described the Natural Law: "true law is right reason in agreement with nature; it is of universal application, unchanging and everlasting".

- St Thomas Aquinas wrote the *Summa Theologica* which summarised and expressed in a systematic form all the knowledge of the time. Aquinas drew extensively on the philosophy of Aristotle and in particular on his Ethics.

- God's guidance of the cosmos may be analysed into four types of laws: (1) the Eternal Law is God's design for creation whereby He upholds the universe in being, and directs things towards their appointed ends; (2) the Natural Law in which God imbues all things with purposes and a striving to fulfil those purposes; (3) the Divine Law whereby God reveals His purposes for mankind in the scriptures and shows how mankind can be made fit to receive divine grace; and (4) the human law, which is created by earthly rulers, and properly construed is a sharing or partnership of humankind with God in His creative work. Human laws therefore should enable us to lead the virtuous life.

- Unfortunately, human acts are not always righteous. Just as individual men and women can sin, so can rulers. In so doing evil rulers exceed their authority and contradict the powers they have been given. Bad laws have no binding power on subjects. We are simply loosed from the bonds of duty in relation to them. In practice, such bad laws do not bind the conscience but we should nevertheless continue to obey them except where to do so would create a greater evil such as lawlessness, scandal or a great harm. But a human law which opposes the Divine plan should never be obeyed.

- Hugo Grotius used Natural Law principles to develop a theory of international law. He set out to discover universally applicable rational principles. He maintained that his Natural Law methods would be equally valid even if there had been no God. An action is good not because it was willed by God but, on the contrary, God would only will those acts which are morally good. In doing so Grotius was expressing the view that Natural Law could be logically independent of theological truths.

- Hobbes had a very pessimistic view of human nature. He thought that in our natural state we are selfish, greedy for power, violent and anarchic. Every man is at war with every other. Life is "solitary, poore, nasty, brutish and short". But, at the same time, every person has a desire for peace.

- Peace and political stability can be achieved only by the creation of a sovereign (whether a person or group of people) who can use the power of law to defend citizens. Hobbes imagines a mythical time when the people appoint a sovereign and enter into a contract with him, making over *all* of their separate powers to him. He will use those powers to impose peace and order upon his kingdom by using the power of law and physical force.

- Under the Social Contract all subjects are made equal. Hobbes thought that a duly appointed paternal sovereign would always act justly. But a ruler who took power by force following a conquest or victory in war could be a despot. In such circumstances the subjects would owe their sovereign no obligations at all, but might overthrow him and kill him.

- Hume believed that the only true knowledge of things was to be arrived at through the perceptions of the senses. In many ways Hume's idea of knowledge acquisition can be likened to a person sitting in a darkened room, viewing the world outside through a window. The whole process of learning about the world is essentially a passive one. Hume's method is often described as empirical since it is based on knowledge of facts acquired through observation, experience and experiment.

- Hume's empirical method suffered from several problems: it could not explain the relation of cause and effect, it could not explain induction, knowledge of the future was impossible. The empirical method could not explain mathematics, aesthetics, religion, law or morality. Hume thought that the only thing that was real about law and morality was the fact that people customarily believed in principles of law and morality and so these legal and moral principles came to affect social behaviour.

- Hume famously held the view that an "ought" of morality could not be derived from an "is" of what is perceived by the senses. Just because human beings do form relationships, procreate and have children does not mean that they *ought* to do so. It seemed that morality was a myth.

- Fuller identifies an "Inner Morality" of law. For rules of morality to be effective in guiding us, there are eight procedural standards to be followed:

  (1) rules must first exist before people can use them for guidance and decision-making;

  (2) rules must be publicised to the parties expected to obey them;

  (3) rules must not be retroactive;

  (4) rules must be understandable;

  (5) rules should not contradict each other;

  (6) rules must not require conduct beyond the ability of the affected party;

  (7) changes must not be so frequent that people cannot orientate themselves to them; and

  (8) there must be a congruence between rules as published and rules as administered.

  A failure in any of these eight standards does not simply create a bad system of law, it fails to create any system of law at all.

- Finnis derived a list of seven "self-evident" basic goods (or "basic forms of human flourishing") which are: life, knowledge, play, aesthetic experience, sociability (friendship), practical reasonableness, and religion (the concern with "questions of cosmic order and of human freedom and reason").

- Finnis's list of self-evident basic goods are said to provide for us all that is good for human individuals given the human nature that we share. The "basic goods" will enable us to lead a good life, make good choices and seek virtue. The law should respect and promote these basic forms of human flourishing, since these will achieve those virtuous ends for individuals, and in addition attain the common good.

3 MORAL THEORIES AND PRACTICAL REASON

We saw in the last chapter that moral principles are necessary for any understanding of Natural Law. We shall now turn to examine some major moral theories. It is important that we recognise them and their strengths and weaknesses. Ultimately, the theories alone will not tell us how to lead a good life. For this practical reason is required. This is a matter of judgement and skill in making the decisions necessary for daily life. The chapter ends with an influential modern example of practical reasoning – that of a prominent Scot, the late Professor Sir Neil MacCormick. MacCormick draws on various ideas and combines them into a powerful contemporary virtue theory which is suitable for both legal and moral decision making. We shall see some of his other ideas in Chapters 4 and 8.

MORAL THEORIES

Moral theories may be roughly divided into four types: virtue theories, duty-based theories, Consequentialist theories and Relativist theories.

Virtue theories

Aristotle starts by looking at the structure of human nature. Man is a rational animal. His decisions are guided by the soul but he is also subject to various drives which emanate from his body. The soul seeks piety and learns and thinks. It is imprisoned within the body. The effect of this is that there are some things of intellectual virtue such as philosophy, mathematics and logic. These studies reveal to us things of eternal value. Forms of decision and behaviour which encourage the ascendancy of the soul over the body will be virtues. It is not entirely clear how to accommodate emotions and senses. Both of these have bodily and mental aspects. However, Aristotle tells us that a man ruled by the soul will seek virtues that are good – the Good Life. This includes such virtues as truth, wisdom, moderation, temperance, justice, courage and politics. All of these can be rationally justified and bring true happiness while following base desires leads along the path of destruction. There also exist things which are less directly good for life, such as discipline, medicine and exercise. In each case these bring about health – ethical and physical. Aristotle also notices that nature (including mankind) appears to have inbuilt purposes or ends (an end is "*telos*" in Greek). Acorns always grow into oak trees. They always seek their appointed end. Human beings should seek virtue or excellence – that is their appointed end. A virtue, then, is not an emotion or feeling but is a disposition or habit and its pursuit involves making appropriate choices in life. The virtues are independent from one another but they appear to have certain characteristics in common – they bring about the good. There is circularity in this argument. Aristotle says that the good life is our appointed end and it is good for us to pursue it. Unfortunately, he does not tell us how to achieve the virtues. In this we should do what a good person does. A virtuous man is an example to the rest. As we live through time, if we have pursued virtue and made virtuous choices, we develop a character which is virtuous. Again, the circularity creeps in. Somehow we should be able to inculcate the good and virtuous for, by our choices, we will be praised or blamed. We are therefore responsible for our acts. Actions which are not free and voluntary may absolve us from responsibility. If we acquire false beliefs and act voluntarily on the strength of them then our actions are misdirected and we may not be held fully responsible for them where our ignorance can be excused. If we are drunk and do things we would not otherwise do, then we will regret them and may escape responsibility for our actions since they may not be fully voluntary.

Despite its faults, mainly lack of specification, there is a certain charm and attraction in Aristotle's virtue ethics. We do tend to know (when we reflect upon them) that our actions are intrinsically right or wrong. And we do make life plans and choices in relation to which some of our choices may be constructive or destructive. But as a system of morality it is simply too vague. When we come to consider MacCormick's practical reasoning, you will find that there are many echoes of Aristotle's virtue ethics.

Duty-based theories

Duty-based theories, sometimes called "deontological theories", again start from the premise that we know that our acts are intrinsically morally right or wrong but the reasoning is different. Under a duty-based theory our actions are right when we do our moral duty, and wrong when we breach our moral duty. Every action of an autonomous moral agent is an opportunity to choose to do the right thing or the wrong. Generally, we should know what is right or wrong in the circumstances. To do this we may have recourse to moral commands or to moral principles. Moral commands are rules which may be expressed in or derived from authoritative texts (often religious texts), while moral principles are recognised by reason. Rules may be precisely specified in words and so any action which does not fall precisely under the description may escape moral evaluation and criticism. Principles are much looser and allow the evaluation of problem cases. We will see in the next chapter that laws may be expressed as rules and principles and also suffer from the same problems of evaluation. Generally, duty-based theories can in their turn be divided into those with religious foundations (Divine Command theories) and those without.

Duties based on religious foundations: Divine Commands

Societies do not develop in a vacuum. Most societies have inherited values derived from religions which are either now or formerly highly influential among the population. In Western nations, most of the values have derived from Christianity which may originally have been imposed under the Canon Law in church courts. Prime among the religious rules are the Ten Commandments handed down by God to Moses (*Exodus*, 20.1–17). These are typical of Divine Commands and form clear, short rules and prohibitions. At one time in history all citizens would have assented to and conformed their behaviour to the Ten Commandments. They are no longer prominent within the law today, but they are probably the origin for some of the criminal law (for example the prohibitions against murder and against theft). There are other Divine Commands, such as the rules of the permitted degrees of consanguinity (*Leviticus*, 18.7–13, 20.17 and 20.19) which continue to inform the law of incest and the laws of marriage. It was early recognised that strict application of rules could lead to problems of interpretation and so systems of interpretation were developed (for example the Jewish Mishnah). In more recent times, judges required to explain and interpret rules and so developed principles of interpretation and provided answers to specific problem situations. Interpretation may enable a body of moral or legal principles to develop. These may acquire general acceptance within the affected societies. Therefore, what may start as individual prohibitions or commands may, through interpretation and necessity, develop into a body of moral rules expressing the culture and values of a people. Eventually the original justifications may become lost in the mists of time. It is arguable that much of Scots criminal law derived from such a development of moral principles but the precise origins of the values are often obscure.

While such moral principles may serve the original community who share the faith, there may be problems for persons who are non-believers. They may have alternative beliefs or none in relation to an issue evaluated by a Divine Command. Unbelievers may question why they should be bound by principles of a religion they do not hold. We may ask whether a religious majority has the right to impose its morality on a non-believing minority. We may also question whether a Divine Command should be imposed unless it achieves some identifiable good end result. There often appears to be a need to loosen the religious bonds and at the same time tighten the obligations of a moral system (which may have grown out of a system of interpreted religious commands). Moral principles may attain general approval if they have a clear utility within the society and are justified on rational rather than religious foundations.

Non-religious duties – Kant and the Categorical Imperative

It is quite possible for there to be rational justifications for moral principles. A very important such theory was devised by Immanuel Kant (1724–1804). He built up a set of moral principles based on the rational acknowledgement of the autonomy of the agent and of other rational beings. All rational agents had an equal right to freedom of action. Kant formulated his theory in a principle known as the "Categorical Imperative". Kant recognised that we live and act within an environment where we encounter both things and persons. Things have no rational purposes of their own and so may be used by us to attain our own desires and fulfil our purposes. Things offer us no resistance to such use. Persons are entirely different. We must recognise that persons have desires and purposes of their own. We would not want them to use us as a mere means to achieve their ends. And it follows that we should equally not be entitled to use them to fulfil our desires and purposes. There is a mutual recognition of the other's status as an autonomous moral being. We have an overriding duty to respect the freedom of other rational people – though there may be situations where a compromise should be reached. It follows from Kant's theory that "it is our duty always to treat people as ends in themselves and never merely as means to an end". This is the first formulation of the Categorical Imperative. This duty is imperative because it commands us and it is categorical because it acknowledges the clear categorical distinction between rational beings with minds of their own and things which have no minds. This is a distinction we know and recognise through our understanding of the world. It is knowledge which is independent of our desires. On the contrary, an imperative would be a hypothetical imperative if it depended upon our desires such as: If you want to do X in circumstances C, then do A. To illustrate this point, imagine a person who wishes to become healthy saying to themselves: "work out for 15 minutes every day in order to become healthy". This is a clear case of a hypothetical imperative. The action is directly related to the purpose. If the agent wants to become healthy then he must do the work-out. It follows that if he no longer wishes to become healthy, then he can cease to follow his rule. But a categorical imperative allows of no such "means to end" relation. It always holds true and no rational being would cease to be under its imperative claim.

There is a second formulation of the Categorical Imperative which stresses the universal quality of the rule. This is formulated as "act only according to that maxim whereby you can at the same time will that it should become a universal law". The idea of universalised principles is very important in practical ethics. Surely if some principle is morally true, then it should have general effect? It must be true at all times and in all places and for all rational beings.

Another feature of Kant's theory is that it insists that moral action is conducted only by morally autonomous beings who are capable of following its dictates. The Categorical Imperative is addressed to such beings: do this and choose your maxims according to whether they can be universalised. We each state this law to ourselves in order to direct our actions. It would make no sense if we were unable to obey the rules we address to ourselves. We are, each of us, autonomous legislators within what Kant calls the "Kingdom of Ends".

Kant's theory is, however, subject to some well-known difficulties. One oddity is that an action is right or wrong only if we recognise and do our duty. It follows that giving money to the poor is morally right if, and only if, we give because we recognise our obligation to provide necessaries to those who cannot provide for themselves. But the same action is not morally right where it arises because we want to be seen by others as doing good. The motive for doing one's duty should always be the desire to obey a categorical rule. No other motive will suffice.

The universalisation of duties can also give rise to some well-known absurdities. One example is known as the "homicidal maniac paradox". Suppose that you have a flatmate with whom you are good friends. One night, your flatmate pops out to the corner shop to buy some cans of beer. When he is out, a homicidal maniac comes to the flat and demands to know where your flatmate is. You know that the maniac wants to kill your friend. What do you do? If speech is to be understood as an activity aimed at transferring true knowledge from one person to another, then you may recognise that you are under a categorical duty to tell the truth at all times. For a Kantian, you have no choice. You have to tell the homicidal maniac that your friend has just popped out to the corner shop and will be back soon. The Kantian must do his duty to tell the truth and is simply not permitted to tell a white lie. This example shows how the idea of doing duty may often bring us into a tension with other descriptions of the action – particularly having regard to its consequences. This conclusion is not restricted to lying but is a general criticism of Kantian duties.

Another feature common to duty-based theories is that every action is inherently right or wrong evaluated by whether we are doing our duty or not. It is assumed that we know precisely what our duties are at the time when we choose to act or not. But this may not be realistic.

Consequentialist theories – Utilitarianism

Consequentialist theories judge an action's moral quality only by whether the action produces good or bad consequences. They state that the end justifies the means.

The most influential of the Consequentialist theories is known as Utilitarianism. This theory, which had its origins in the writings of Plato, became best known in the formulation given by Jeremy Bentham (1748–1832). Bentham said that we should strive to produce "the greatest good for the greatest number." The theory is loosely based on Bentham's analysis of human nature which he thought was motivated by our experience and expectation of pleasures and pains. He writes:

> "nature has placed mankind under the governance of two sovereign masters, pain and pleasure. It is for them alone to point out what we ought to do, as well as to determine what we shall do. On the one hand the standard of right and wrong, on the other the chain of causes and effects, are fastened to their throne. They govern us in all we do, in all we say, in all we think".

We instinctively do what brings us pleasure and we avoid what brings us pain. All our actions involve a sort of balancing act in which we calculate the likely consequences of our actions and choose the best course of action – in the sense of the course of action which produces the greatest amount of pleasure or the least amount of pain. Bentham called the weighing up of pleasures and pains, the "felicific calculus".

Bentham recognised that pains and pleasures come in many different forms. He stated that there are categories of intensity, duration, certainty, proximity, productiveness, purity and extent. But there remain enormous problems for such a theory. How do we balance different pleasures and pains against each other? This is like weighing up chalk and cheese. In some cases we may have to weigh unquantifiable benefits against quantifiable pains. Better education costs money. The payment of how much extra tax equates with how much improvement in education? These are the sorts of issues that politicians have to make in drawing up political policy. They often resort to Utilitarian arguments of one sort or another but getting the correct balance is difficult, if not impossible.

Other problems include the fact that we often do not know what the future will actually produce. We have only our prediction of it. How do we evaluate our actions if we try, but fail, to bring about an intended good? Is our action wrong if it happens to produce pains but fails to produce the anticipated benefits?

Even the comment "the greatest good for the greatest number" is subject to ambiguity, for should we be trying to maximise the amount of good, even if only a few people will share in it, or should we be trying to maximise the number of people who can experience the good, even if the amount of good they each gain may be small or even insignificant?

Another striking problem concerns Utilitarianism's failure to take individuals seriously. The theory tends to look only at the common good. Supposing that three people escape from a sinking ship and are cast adrift with no food. Are they justified in killing one of their number so that the others can eat the deceased? From a Utilitarian viewpoint, the greatest good for the greatest number should prevail. The killing and eating of a crew member is justified by the preservation of the life of the others. But we would recoil from this suggestion. We tend to regard the moral quality of killing as being essentially evil. A Utilitarian justification is not sufficient to make sense of our intuitions. Utilitarian justifications appear again in Chapter 10 where we look at punishment. In that context we shall see that Utilitarianism can justify the punishment of proxies (such as relatives or children of wrongdoers) instead of the actual wrongdoer who deserves the punishment. What is important in the Utilitarian analysis is that the end (say, of deterrence) is achieved.

Since Bentham there have been a number of notable scholars who have advanced Utilitarian theories. One such was John Stuart Mill who reformulated the principle of utility in a number of ways in order to avoid some of the above difficulties. One such change concerns the meaning of happiness which is achieved. It is not the happiness of the individual act that is involved but ultimate happiness, the achieving of the common good. Mill says:

"happiness is the test of all rules of conduct, and the end of life. But I now thought that this end was only to be attained by not making it the direct end. Those only are happy (I thought) who have their minds fixed upon some object other than their own happiness; on the happiness of others, on the improvement of mankind, even on some pursuit, followed not as a means, but as itself an ideal end. Aiming thus at something else, they find happiness on the way ... the only chance is to treat, not happiness, but some end external to it, as the purpose of life".

But in what do these ideal ends consist? Mill also emphasised the importance of individual liberty which justice should strive to protect. He said that the only justification of crime and punishment and for civil actions for damages was where one party had done harm to another (the "harm principle"). In such circumstances, a party has a moral as well as a legal claim on the state to defend him. Injustice is taking or withholding from a citizen a claim to which the citizen has a moral right. Injustice produces resentment. We need the perpetrator to be punished or make reparation.

Another improvement to Utilitarianism involves the distinction between Act-Utilitarianism and Rule-Utilitarianism. Act-Utilitarianism involves the assessment of the quality of an individual act and approves of it if it brings about the greater good. Rule-Utilitarianism justifies the imposition of a rule which, if followed, will bring about the greater good. An example of this is a prohibition against crossing a lawn in a park rather than going round the grass by means of a path. If everyone acted according to Act-Utilitarianism then everyone would conduct the evaluative balancing act and decide whether to cross the grass or go round by the path. Soon the grass would show signs of wear. This would not achieve the end of preserving the lawn. However, under a Rule-Utilitarian approach, the park authorities could impose a general rule that "no-one is to cross the grass". Although the grass would not be damaged if only one or two people crossed it, the prohibition, as a rule of general applicability, applies to all. If all follow the rule, then the lawn will remain pristine. In law, it is not uncommon for rules to be justified upon Rule-Utilitarian grounds.

The above criticisms of Utilitarianism tend to apply to all Consequentialist theories.

Relativist theories

Relativist theories assume that there are no hard and fast moral principles or rules. Instead, we must carry out our evaluation of the moral quality of the act at the time of the decision and on the basis of all the criteria we consider relevant at the time. Different cultures and different ages will have their own culturally relative views on evaluation. Moral codes reflect such cultural relativity. As a result, while, in Western nations, the idea of monogamy is encouraged as a significant value (to the extent that bigamy and polygamy are criminalised), this need not be the case in other cultures or at other times. For this reason polygamy is practised as a morally and legally acceptable form of marriage in Muslim nations. Even in the United States there was a time when polygamy was allowed within Mormon communities (to avoid the danger of the faith dying out), though it is generally frowned upon today.

Relativist theories suggest that moral values can change. In most societies, the changes are usually slow and incremental rather than rapid and wide ranging. Indeed, this would have to be the case for the principles to be capable of being used by members of the society for guiding and informing their moral choices. A society which had rapid and wide-ranging changes would not have the ability to guide and inform citizens nor would the society have the appearance of following moral principles.

Within a Relativist society, one may therefore expect principles and rules to develop through time and possibly to lose authority and finally cease to exist. It may be suggested that this situation characterises our own society and its laws. There are many instances of slow changes in attitudes which may produce law reform (or even be brought about by law reform). One example would be the prohibition against driving a motor vehicle while under the influence of alcohol or drugs. Before s 4(1) of the Road Traffic Act 1988 was enacted, people frequently went to pubs in their cars and drove home again afterwards even when materially impaired by alcohol. Since the prohibition, arguably it may now be said to be immoral as well as illegal to drive home from a pub after having a drink. Everyone knows the risks involved and many right-thinking people would regard themselves as being under a duty to inform the authorities if they became aware of a drunk person getting behind the wheel of a car.

MacCORMICK ON PRACTICAL REASON

In *Practical Reason in Law and Morality*, Neil MacCormick, the late Regius Professor of Law at Edinburgh University, set out to explain how good decisions are to be achieved in everyday life. He doubted that it is possible for free and autonomous individuals to make decisions based upon moral theories alone. He said:

"in practice, as is obvious every day conscientious and reasonable people thinking rationally and reasonably about moral issues do come to different and mutually incompatible, sometimes sharply opposed, conclusions. Issues about drugs, about euthanasia, and about abortion are no more than especially vivid illustrations of this. So we may conclude about morality: morality is both discursive and controversial because it presupposes the autonomy of all who take it seriously".

We do not act on the basis of pure reason alone. In common with all other human beings, we have emotions. These cause us to feel empathy for others. When they are in pain we sympathise with them. When they are joyful we are happy with them. Like them, we are motivated by feelings of joy, love, gratitude and pleasure. And we also seek aesthetic pleasures such as natural beauty, art, music and architecture. Emotions are very important as motives for our actions. The Enlightenment Edinburgh philosopher David Hume realised the importance of emotions as reasons for action. He noticed that we are much more motivated by our emotions than by our faculty of reason. He said: "reason is, and ought only to be the slave of the passions, and can never pretend to any other office than to serve and obey them". MacCormick considered that our feelings of empathy towards our neighbours can act as a control over our basic passions. He said: "practical reasoning is not an oxymoron. It can be directed at all self-regarding, other-regarding, and community-regarding reasons, having as their content human goods that are either animal or ideal in character".

To understand the role that such empathy has when it comes to social action, MacCormick derives support from Adam Smith and Kant. Smith tells us that we are not mere impartial observers. We reflect upon the emotional expressions of others and upon our own empathy for them. When we see good deeds and their positive results, we are pleased. When we see evil acts and their negative effects, we are shocked. Just as we approve or disapprove of the conduct of others, so we learn to approve or disapprove of our own good and evil actions. Thus, by reflection, we develop a faculty of moral judgement. This provides a basis not only for self-criticism but also for moral judgment. Thus, according to MacCormick, we "get from sympathy with others' pain and distress to moral approval and disapproval".

This is not yet enough. MacCormick considers that Kant's moral philosophy plays a vital part in explaining our moral choices. The Categorical Imperative tells us that we must never treat others as means for our own projects, but to respect them only as ends in themselves. In its other formulation we are told that we should will only that which we would wish to be a universal maxim of action. MacCormick combines both these formulations of the Categorical Imperative with Smith's empathic criticism of the self to form what MacCormick calls "a Smithian Categorical Imperative".

MacCormick formulates this into two imperatives. The principal imperative states:

> "enter as fully as you can into the feelings of everyone directly involved in and affected by an incident or relationship, and impartially form a maxim of judgment about what is right that all could accept if they were committed to maintaining mutual beliefs setting a common standard of approval and disapproval among themselves."

The subsidiary imperative is:

> "act in accordance with that impartial judgement of what it is right to do in respect of the given incident or relationship".

Another important feature of Kant's moral philosophy is the idea that every individual is a free and autonomous moral agent who is a "law unto himself". The importance of this is that we are not always free in our actions. MacCormick gives the example of Odysseus who "failed to sail home directly after the Greeks' final victory at Troy ... not because of any decision he made but because of a contrary wind that forced his ship off course while sailing homewards. Mariners under sail are at the mercy of the wind". In the same way, human beings "suffer forms of psychological compulsion, phobias, and the like" which prevent them from acting with full autonomy. In these circumstances their actions fail to be fully moral.

MacCormick then proceeds to analyse forms of practical relationship with other human beings. To do this he adopts ideas from the writings of Stair. In the *Institutions of the Law of Scotland* Stair advances three basic practical principles of equity which he calls obedience, freedom and engagement. MacCormick says that these delineate our practical reason. Regarding obedience, MacCormick says that there are basic interpersonal duties which we must observe (such as that we must not kill or injure others). One must always fulfil one's basic duties. Beyond that, one is morally free to do as one thinks best. Freedom may be limited by voluntarily making engagements (promises, contracts, etc) with others. MacCormick asserts that there is "virtue in doing one's duty and being a conscientious person". Only after one has given due weight to one's obedience can one then recognise our actions as being free. Freedom for MacCormick means that "we have freedom in the sense of normative liberty wherever no duty exists or applies. We are free to deliberate among whatever seems to us discernible courses of action and in a large way we are morally free to construct and periodically revise our own plan of life, just so long as we do not plan to infringe the basic duties". Within these limits, we are free to carry out our decisions and fulfil our plans and projects. As rational moral agents we act for reasons, and we do this in a fully rational way only if we recognise all our reasons, strike a practical balance among them, and apply them in doing what is best in the circumstances.

Our actions do not occur in a vacuum. At all times we reflect upon our actions and those of others. We criticise our and their reasons and motives. This is where the second formulation of Kant's Categorical Imperative becomes important. Through time we develop universal principles and maxims of action. We learn to describe actions as "right" or "wrong". In this way our moral choices can come to be described in terms of universal rules for action that guide us.

Having explained his view of practical reason, MacCormick then shows how we may apply the Smithian Categorical Imperative within the fields of law and morality. In the field of law, we observe rules concerning our basic duties (not to kill or harm others), we can enter into contracts and engagements with others ("to enable social coherence and commerce"), and we can learn to judge justly. In this way, within the field of law we aim to promote "society, property and commerce" just as Stair states.

Turning to the field of morality, MacCormick brings us back to and fleshes out his version of virtue ethics. We aim for a good life so that we may stay alive, secure a livelihood for oneself and dependants, and create meaningful life-plans. His conclusion is worth stating in full:

> "a person leads a good life, and makes the best of her or his chances, by seeking to realise in reasonable ways and with independence of judgment some element or part of the good, and, over time, some balanced mix of different goods whose pursuit is mutually compatible. Each needs some overall view of his or her life and its direction or trajectory through time, here somewhat grandiloquently entitled 'a life plan'. In such a plan, intrinsically worthwhile aims and objectives are conceived and adopted as ends, acknowledging that there are auxiliary virtues that have to be cultivated for successful pursuit of these. As well as independence of mind one has to develop self-knowledge, courage, reasonableness, technological competence, considerateness for others, politeness, self-respect without selfishness, diligence and a will to hard work, along with patience in the face of adversity and ill luck. These are virtues one can try to develop while at the same time pursuing some of

the goods wrapped up under such headings as life and health, education and learning, good communications, aesthetic values, religious experience and activity, recreational activities, friendship and political activity. These goods thus delineated do not amount to a complete or definitive list, though surely nothing that directly conflicts with any of them would find a due place in the expanded list."

Essential concepts

- **Moral** theories may be roughly divided into four types: virtue theories, duty-based theories, Consequentialist theories and Relativist theories.

- **Virtue** theories look at the structure of human nature and in particular note that we are rational animals. Aristotle thought that we had a rational mind but were subject to bodily drives. Reason reveals things of eternal value. Forms of decision and behaviour which encourage the ascendancy of the soul over the body will be virtues.

  - The goal of mankind is to seek excellence and strive for the good life. In doing this we learn virtues which are good dispositions or habits. Aristotle names a number of virtues: truth, wisdom, moderation, temperance, justice, courage and politics.

  - Virtues can be rationally justified and bring true happiness. Following base desires brings destruction.

  - There are also indirect goods for life such as discipline, medicine and exercise. In each case these bring about health – ethical and physical.

  - Living the virtuous life means learning habitually to make appropriate choices in life.

  - Aristotle says that the good life is our appointed end and it is good for us to pursue it. He does not tell us how to achieve the virtues. In this we should look to what a good person does to guide us.

  - We are responsible for our acts. Actions which are not free and voluntary may absolve us from responsibility.

  - Aristotle's virtue ethics lacks detail and suffers from circularity.

- In a **duty-based** theory our actions are right when we do our moral duty, and wrong when we breach our moral duty. Every action of an autonomous moral agent is an opportunity to choose to do the right thing or the wrong. Generally, we should know what is right or wrong in the circumstances.

  - Divine Command theories derive moral rules and principles from religious texts or religious beliefs. The Ten Commandments are an example of divine commands.

  - Strict application of rules could lead to problems when they are applied to unexpected circumstances. As a result, systems of interpretation may be required. Interpretation may enable a body of moral or legal principles to develop. Moral principles are more generalised and so produce fewer problems in unexpected situations. These may acquire general acceptance within the affected societies.

  - While moral principles may serve the original community who share the faith, there may be problems for persons who are non-believers. They may have alternative beliefs or none in relation to an issue evaluated by a Divine Command. Unbelievers may question why they should be bound by principles of a religion they do not hold.

  - Moral principles may attain general approval if they have a clear utility within the society and are justified on rational rather than religious foundations.

  - Kant thought that it is quite possible for there to be purely rational justifications for moral principles. Kant formulated the "Categorical Imperative". We must recognise that persons have desires and purposes of their own.

  - In the first formulation of the Categorical Imperative "it is our duty always to treat people as ends in themselves and never merely as means to an end".

  - The second formulation of the Categorical Imperative stresses the universal quality of a moral rule. We should "act only according to that maxim whereby you can at the same time will that it should become a universal law".

  - Kant insisted that moral action is conducted only by morally autonomous beings who are capable of following its dictates.

It is assumed that we always know what our duty is. But this may not be realistic.

○ Kant's theory is, however, subject to some well-known, difficulties. One oddity is that an action is right or wrong only if we recognise and do our duty.

○ The universalisation of duties can also give rise to some well-known absurdities. One example is known as the "homicidal maniac paradox".

• **Consequentialist** theories judge an action's moral quality only by whether the action produces good or bad consequences. The end justifies the means.

○ Utilitarianism is the most influential of the consequentialisms. This seeks to produce "the greatest good for the greatest number". Our choices are governed by pleasures and pains. We instinctively do what brings us pleasure and we avoid what brings us pain. In deciding whether an action is good we must weigh up the pleasures and pains. This is known as the "felicific calculus".

○ There are many problems for Utilitarianism. How do we balance different pleasures and pains against each other? We often do not know what the future consequences of our actions will be. The rule "the greatest good for the greatest number" is ambiguous. Are we trying to maximise the greatest good or the greatest number of people to share it? Utilitarian arguments stress the common good but often fail to give justice to the individual.

○ Mill thought that true happiness only occurs where people have their minds fixed upon some object other than their own happiness: on the happiness of others, on the improvement of mankind, even on some pursuit, followed not as a means, but as itself an ideal end.

○ Mill also emphasised the importance of individual liberty which justice should strive to protect. Injustice is taking or withholding from a citizen a claim to which the citizen has a moral right. We need the perpetrator to be punished or make reparation.

- o Act-Utilitarianism involves the assessment of the quality of an individual act and approves of it if it brings about the greater good.
- o Rule-Utilitarianism justifies the imposition of a rule which, if followed in every case, will bring about the greater good. In law, it is not uncommon for rules to be justified upon Rule-Utilitarian grounds.
- o Utilitarian arguments are very useful. Politicians often resort to Utilitarian arguments in setting policy.

- **Relativist** theories assume that there are no hard and fast moral principles or rules. Different cultures and different ages will have their own culturally relative views on evaluation. Moral codes reflect such cultural relativity.

  - o Relativist theories suggest that moral values can change. In most societies, changes are usually slow and incremental rather than rapid and wide ranging.

- **Neil MacCormick** doubts that it is possible for free and autonomous individuals to make decisions based upon moral theories alone. What is needed is a form of virtue ethics.

  - o We do not act on the basis of pure reason alone. David Hume said: "reason is, and ought only to be the slave of the passions, and can never pretend to any other office than to serve and obey them". Our moral choices involve our emotions.

  - o We feel empathy for others. When they are in pain, we sympathise with them. When they are joyful, we are happy with them. When we see good deeds and their positive results, we are pleased. When we see evil acts and their negative effects, we are shocked. Just as we approve or disapprove of the conduct of others, so we learn to approve or disapprove of our own good and evil actions. This can provide the basis for moral judgement.

  - o MacCormick considers that Kant's moral philosophy plays a vital part in explaining our moral choices. MacCormick approves of the Categorical Imperative, of Kant's insistence that a moral agent is free and autonomous, and that a moral rule should have universal application. By combining the idea of empathy with Kant's moral thinking, MacCormick formulates two imperatives.

o The principal imperative states: "enter as fully as you can into the feelings of everyone directly involved in and affected by an incident or relationship, and impartially form a maxim of judgment about what is right that all could accept if they were committed to maintaining mutual beliefs setting a common standard of approval and disapproval among themselves".

o The subsidiary imperative is: "act in accordance with that impartial judgement of what it is right to do in respect of the given incident or relationship".

o MacCormick says that there are three basic practical principles of equity which he calls obedience, freedom and engagement and which define our practical reason. We must first obey our basic interpersonal duties (such as that we must not kill or injure others). Beyond that, one is morally free to do as one thinks best.

o In our daily lives we may voluntarily limit our freedom by making engagements (promises, contracts, etc) with others.

o Through time we develop universal principles and maxims of action. We learn to describe actions as "right" or "wrong". In this way our moral choices can come to be described in terms of universal rules for action that guide us.

o As free moral agents we must strike a practical balance among our moral maxims and apply them in doing what is best.

o MacCormick shows how we may apply his practical reasoning within the fields of law and morality.

o In the field of morality, we aim for a good life so that we may stay alive, secure a livelihood for oneself and dependants, and create meaningful life-plans.

4 LEGAL POSITIVISM

In Chapter 2 we saw that Contractarianism arose as a means of controlling mankind's natural state of lawlessness. Hobbes's Contractarianism emphasised the crucial role of a sovereign in creating a legal system which would guarantee peace and stability and individual freedoms. This was one element in the development of classical Legal Positivism. Another element was Hume's rejection of objective morality. All was ultimately a matter of custom.

These two ideas were united in classical Legal Positivism which was propounded by Jeremy Bentham (1748–1832). He was a great pamphleteer who rejected any form of Natural Law. It is this that provides the definition of Positivism which is any system of law which rejects a necessary connection between law and morality. Bentham's rejection of morality is very reminiscent of Hume. He wrote: "To the province of the expositor belongs to explain to us what ... the law is: to that of the censor, to observe what he thinks it ought to be." In this way Bentham divides the "is" of the law from the "ought" of its moral content. Bentham then sets out the expositorial view. Unfortunately, much of Bentham's work in this area became lost and was not rediscovered until the late 20th century. While acknowledging the debt due to Bentham, it is usual to examine the somewhat more rigorous theory put forward by Bentham's pupil, John Austin (1790–1859).

After examining Austin's views, we shall look at some modern forms of Legal Positivism. Broadly, Legal Positivism takes the view that the validity of law depends on its sources and not its merits. While not denying that morality may have a place, Positivists deny that there is any necessary connection between law and morality. For Austin and Kelsen, authority comes from a sovereign or political power and is distributed through the law. But Hart takes a different view and places the authority of law into the hands of the people who form society.

AUSTIN'S "COMMAND THEORY"

John Austin agreed with Hume's "is"/"ought" distinction:

> "The existence of the law is one thing, its merit or demerit is another. Whether it be or be not is one enquiry, whether it be or be not conformable to an assumed standard, is a different enquiry. A law which actually exists,

is a law, though we happen to dislike it, or though it vary from the text, by which we regulate our approbation or disapprobation." (*Lecture V,* p 157)

Austin defined a law as a command of a sovereign:

> "1. A wish or desire conceived by a rational being, that another rational being shall do or forbear. 2. An evil to proceed from the former, and to be incurred by the latter, in case the latter comply not with the wish. 3. An expression or intimation of the wish by words or other signs."

That is to say that a law is a wish of the sovereign expressed as a command addressed to the subject and, in the event of the subject's failure to comply, the imposition of a sanction or punishment of some sort. There are therefore three essential elements to a law as a command: (1) sovereign, (2) subject, and (3) sanction. It has to be noted that we are here dealing with the use of political power which has its source in the sovereign and which is wielded against the subject and that this results in pressure on the subject to obey and coercion if he does not.

Part of Austin's project is to show that this definition is correct for all forms of law. He uses this three-part definition to show how the rules of morality and custom on the one hand, and the laws of science as demonstrated in nature on the other, do not form "laws properly so called". These lack one or more of the elements. Rules of morality and custom are "laws by analogy" but lack a sovereign or the imposition of a sanction. Laws of nature are "laws by metaphor", which explains the regularity of nature but of course there is no intelligence at work.

With regard to the "laws properly so called", these comprise the laws of God to men which men must obey or they will suffer punishment in Hell (clearly, here, all of sovereign, command, intelligent subject and sanction are involved); and the "laws of men to men" which fall to be divided up, apparently into two further categories: "laws strictly so called" being commands made by a political sovereign to political subjects in pursuance of legal rights and duties; and "laws not strictly so called" being rules made by men but not as political sovereigns (for example the rules made by parents and to be obeyed by children or by clubs over their members). These are arguably law-like and have all the elements. We shall now look at certain of Austin's elements in turn.

Command

The essence of command is some sign, performance or statement by the sovereign which serves to communicate a wish and which is backed up with a sanction for failure in performance:

"If you express or intimate a wish that I shall do or forbear from some act, and if you will visit me with an evil in case I comply not with our wish, the expression or intimation of your wish is a command. A command is distinguished from other significations of desire not by the style in which the desire is signified, but by the power and the purpose of the party commanding to inflict an evil or a pain in case the desire be disregarded."

The importance of the utterer being sovereign and the importance of the sanction are that the command should be authoritative and powerful. Only the sovereign has the power to enforce their command. They, and only they, have the legitimate right to use force. Austin explains the authority of the law as arising because of its origins and use of political power. This inculcates in us the habit of obedience: given that the sovereign is legitimate and powerful we are bound to obey – with force if need be. But when we look closely at this, we find some problems. Are all laws commands in this sense? There are some obvious exceptions. For example, where do we place international laws? Are these not the expressions of the wishes of sovereigns? Are these not interpreted and enforced in courts? But, of course, they may have no sanction attached to them. Strictly, they fail to meet Austin's definition of "law". There are also many other areas of the law which have no apparent sanction attached, for example laws which allow for the creation and regulation of contracts. Austin recognises the difficulty but thinks that a sanction is still potentially present. Is there not a sanction of a sort when a court enforces a breach of contract: when the party who has breached will either have to pay damages or be compelled by the courts to fulfil their contractual obligations?

Sovereign

It is very important to Austin that the sovereign should be the source of all political power (for this is what any Contractarian view supports) and the only party who may legitimately use force. It follows from this that no other party may issue authoritative commands and also that the sovereign should be subject to no other authority. Austin expresses it in this way:

"The sovereign is not in a habit of obedience to a determinate superior ... it follows from ... the nature of sovereignty and independent political society, that the power ... of a sovereign ... in its ... sovereign capacity, is incapable of legal limitation. A sovereign ... bound by a legal duty, [would be] ... subject to a higher or superior sovereign ... supreme power limited by positive law, is a flat contradiction in terms."

From a political point of view, a sovereign is the person (or indeed it could be a collection of persons) who makes the commands (laws). It is the state's legislature. As the sovereign has unrestricted power, it follows that in the Austinian state, the legislature may make laws on any subject and over any territory. This gives rise to the idea of unbounded sovereignty. Austin's concept of sovereignty cannot accommodate the direct effect of some EU regulatory law and of European case law. Indeed, so persuasive is the Austinian idea of sovereignty that even today there are those in government who experience the idea of Europe as a contradiction with a proper understanding of the sovereignty of the Queen in Parliament.

Sanction

It is not enough that a law should simply be wished: it must be commanded. Obedience is not optional. Austin's answer to the habit of obedience that characterises the majority of subjects is that the command is enforced by a sanction if need be: "it is the power and the purpose of inflicting eventual evil, and not the power and the purpose of imparting eventual good, which gives to the expression of a wish the name of a command". In Austin's view this gives an adequate explanation for the authority of all laws. A sanction is a punishment, a deprivation, or other form of harm, pain or other evil. We may wish to ask ourselves why Austin thinks that the law's authority has to be explained in this way. The use of a threatened sanction will create powerful psychological motives for obedience and can be justified on Utilitarian grounds (which Austin would have approved of) but it detracts from a picture of law as a benevolent and ordered structure. It may command many things but it does not command our respect. In some ways the Command Theory sets out to provide a value neutral view of law, but it actually presents us with a rather pessimistic view of law: one where force is the only foundation for authority. Is there not another way?

Hart's criticisms of the Command Theory

Hart, in *The Concept of Law*, has four criticisms of the Command Theory:

- Law as the Austinian command of a sovereign, is like the demands of a gunman who points a gun at a bank clerk and orders the clerk to hand over money otherwise he will be shot. The Austinian view of coercion is abhorrent – it is a demand with menaces. Such a view is unable to make us feel that the law has authority. The law's authority must arise in a different way. Furthermore, law makes general demands which apply to all people within the society and even applies to those making the demand, to the legislators.

- Many laws do not impose duties but provide means whereby citizens are empowered to carry out certain kinds of acts such as making contracts, making wills, getting married, and so on. In these cases people take advantage of opportunities that the law provides. They harness its power. It is enabling.

- It is incorrect to say that laws are commands of the sovereign, as a good deal of law has been derived from custom. This is particularly so when one considers the common law as imposed in the courts. Particularly in England, the common law is a body of law which has been built up by equitable court decisions over hundreds of years. Such sources of law have nothing to do with a sovereign making commands.

- Austin's unlimited sovereignty free from legal or other constraint fails to provide an adequate account of how one sovereign can succeed from another. Strictly, when one sovereign dies then, if Austin is correct, the whole system of law collapses. Without a sovereign there can be no law: there is no-one to command the commands. Austin explains the continuity of law by the fiction of "tacit consent": that it continues because it is tacitly adopted by the successor. But there are other ways to explain the continuity of law.

Hart, having attacked the Command Theory, proceeds to build his own important theory, to which we shall return below. However, the Austinian explanation of law as command, containing a necessary relation of three elements (sovereign, subject and sanction), remained the most influential view of law for about two centuries and must therefore be given respect – if for nothing else, then as a formidable opponent.

KELSEN AND THE "PURE THEORY OF LAW"

Hans Kelsen (1881–1973) puts forward an important and influential modern form of Positivism. His view is Positivist because its makes a clear distinction between the law and morality. He does not use Hume's distinction between "is" and "ought" but nonetheless Kelsen rejects all matters that are metaphysical (matters of value of which morality is one). Kelsen is asking "What is the law?" rather than "What ought the law to be?". He sets out to produce a pure science of law. His first step, then, is to strip away from law all extraneous and not strictly legal material which adulterates it and hides its true nature. It is not just morality which must be stripped away from law but also any sociological, psychological or political elements. He writes:

> "adulteration is understandable, because [these] disciplines deal with subject matters that are closely connected with law. The pure theory of law undertakes to delimit the cognition of law against these disciplines, not because it ignores or denies the connection, but because it wishes to avoid the uncritical mixture of methodologically different disciplines … which obscure the essence of the science of law and obliterate the limits imposed upon it by the nature of its subject matter".

The end result of this cleansing is to produce unadulterated law which may then be easier to analyse.

Once cleansed, law still appears to contain rules which say what ought to happen. But this time it is an "ought" of legal force and consequences rather than an "ought" of morality. That is to say, a law is a general statement that says what people "ought" to do in given circumstances. Kelsen calls such laws "norms" and the laws are therefore "normative". The word "norm" comes from the Greek word for a set-square against which right angles would be tested. Laws primarily set a standard of behaviour which people should follow. This is their essence. But it has nothing to do with morality. The logical formula of a norm is: if X, then Y (if circumstances X occur, then do action Y). But norms are not merely addressed to the public, they are also addressed to officials. They authorise and instruct officials to inflict a punishment or take some other remedial action if a member of the public fails to perform the action they should. The formula for this is: if X, then Y; if not-Y then Z (if circumstances X occur, then do action Y, and if action Y is not done, then the appointed official should do action Z). In this way, when there is a rule which says I should stop at a red traffic light and I do not, then an official should give me a penalty or take me to court or take some other enforcement action. The efficacy of the law is causal. According to my response to the norm, certain consequences should causally follow: either compliance or sanction. A properly described norm will make it clear to whom the general rule is addressed, what circumstances it applies to, what action is required, which official is addressed in the event of my failure of compliance, and what action they should take. This is an ambitious set of requirements for any law. A norm is, then, a command (or a permission) which has the power of the state and which states what ought to happen, and harnesses the power of the state to ensure that it has the desired legal effect. People obey the laws primarily because they fear the imposition of the sanction. Sanctions come in various forms.

The most characteristic is the criminal law which imposes punishments. Kelsen notes that punishments are most effective when they relate to things we consider of value: our life, liberty, health and property. But criminal laws are not the only form of sanction. Under the civil law it is unpleasant consequences which may force us to comply with a norm. He writes: "the law is a decree of a measure of coercion, a sanction, for that conduct called illegal, delict; and this conduct has the character of a delict because it is a condition of the sanction". A legal system has continuing legitimacy because it has effectiveness in the sense that the system is accepted by a majority of citizens and, even if it is disobeyed, the official who must impose the sanction will accept the duties the law creates. However, individual norms may cease to have effectiveness. They may cease to be accepted by the majority of citizens; indeed, they may cease to be accepted by officials too. In this case there is an insufficiency of adherence. This gives rise to the phenomenon of desuetude whereby individual norms may come to cease to be recognised and obeyed.

It will be seen that, behind every law, the state is represented by an official who is entitled to use coercion to ensure that the public performs what is required of them and will impose a sanction if it is not. In normative parlance, the norm creates two duties: one on the member of the public to which it is addressed, and the other on the appropriate official. At the same time, norms are rooted in social contexts which they address. These contexts are not impurities which adulterate the law, but rather provide norms with their legal meaning. The persons under obligation, either public or official, understand the legal meanings in these contexts. Kelsen gives some examples of these meanings:

> "if you analyse any body of facts interpreted as 'legal' or somehow tied up with law, such as a parliamentary discussion, an administrative act, a judgment, a contract, or a crime, two elements are distinguishable: one, an act or series of acts – a happening occurring at a certain time and in a certain place, perceived by our senses: an external manifestation of human conduct; two, the legal meaning of this act, that is, the meaning conferred upon the act by the law. For example: People assemble in a large room, make speeches, some raise their hands, others do not – this is the external happening. Its meaning is that a statute is being passed, that law is created. We are faced here with a distinction (familiar to jurists) between the process of legislation and its product, the statute. To give other illustrations: a man in a robe and speaking from a dais says some words to a man standing before him; legally this external happening means: a judicial decision was passed. A merchant writes a letter of a certain content to another merchant, who in turn, answers with a letter; this means they have concluded a legally binding contract. Somebody causes the death of somebody else; legally, this means murder".

Each case has an external and an internal view. On the external view, there is an action, a piece of behaviour: this may describe the event but only partially – it does not provide the legal meaning. On the internal view, an action takes place in a context which is subjectively understood by the participants and they will therefore understand the legal meaning of the situation.

Norms, being the will of the state, fill what might otherwise be semantically empty circumstances with legal meanings. They create legal possibilities. At the same time they have the coercive power of the state behind them designed to ensure compliance and effectiveness. A number of things follow from this. First, as acts of state, norms have authority and validity. Second, as prescriptions of what should be done by individuals and officials, norms force compliance – they create rules which are followed – which have efficacy (which simply means that they are obeyed). Third, norms give circumstances their particular meanings. Fourth, only the state has the authority to use force – which means that other uses of force are invalid. Kelsen gives an example of an unauthorised use of force – the gangster example:

> "The command of a gangster to hand over a certain amount of money has the same subjective meaning as the command of an income tax official, namely that the individual at whom the command is directed ought to pay something. But only the command of the official, not that of the gangster, has the meaning of a valid norm, binding upon the addressed individual. Only the one order, not the other, is a norm-positing act, because the official's act is authorized by a tax law, whereas the gangster's act is not based on such an authorizing norm."

Having described the way that individual norms operate, Kelsen turns his attention to the nature of laws as part of an inter-related system. He asks what it is that gives validity to norms. In the case of a tax official being validly authorised to demand payment, the answer is that there is a norm which authorises the payment. But this norm is not valid on its own. It relies on other norms of more general application. And those in their turn will be validated by yet other norms of even more general content. Kelsen describes a norm which has effect upon a citizen and regulating his or her actions as "concretised". It has meaning and effect in a concrete, actual specific context. The higher norms are more general. Kelsen describes the system of norms as a hierarchy of norms. Ultimately, our quest for validity will take us to the norms of most general effect. For us, in the United Kingdom, this will most likely be actions of the Queen in Parliament, but Kelsen considered that our search would take us to a constitution which he describes as a general norm. He defines the whole system of law as: "a system of coercion imposing norms which are laid down by human acts in accordance with a constitution the validity of which is presupposed if it is on the whole efficacious". Laws all have validity derived from the constitution but they may come into existence in various ways. Kelsen says: "Norms either arise through custom, as do the norms of common law, or are enacted by conscious acts of certain organisations aiming to create law, as does a legislature acting in its law-making capacity."

Kelsen then asks the question what it is that gives validity to the constitution: what is the basis of this general norm? This is a difficult question. Kelsen says that it is "not a norm posited by a real act of will – but a norm presupposed in a believer's thinking". Kelsen calls this presupposition of validity a "*Grundnorm*" (or the basic norm). He says: "the *Grundnorm* really exists in the juristic consciousness [it] is the result of a simple analysis of actual juristic statements. The *Grundnorm* is the answer to the question: how – and that means under what condition – are these juristic statements concerning legal norms – legal duties, legal rights, and so on, possible?" The *Grundnorm* is "by and large" efficacious. It is believed in, given effect to as a matter of general course. It is unquestioned by the members of the society. The *Grundnorm* is the reason why the law "ought" to be obeyed. It is the ultimate source of political power and of the authority of the state. It is very important for Kelsen's view of law. It ends our search for validity. But it is not like other norms. It is not expressed and has no content. Kelsen describes it as follows: "The basic norm is ... not a product of free invention. It refers to particular facts existing in natural reality, to an actually laid down and effective constitution and to the norm creating and norm applying facts established in conformity with the constitution." It is in this sense that it is said to be "presupposed". As to its origin, Kelsen says that it is historical, for norms should be carried out only in the way and under the conditions "determined by the 'fathers' of the constitution or the organs delegated by them". But the *Grundnorm* is not logically connected with the political content of the state which is constituted under it. The norms under the *Grundnorm* may have any content and make any demands on people. In this sense the *Grundnorm* has no content. It is, however, the source of political power and so the source of the coercive power of the state and the law: "The function of the basic norm is not to make it possible to consider a coercive order which is by and large effective as law, for ... a legal order is a coercive order by and large effective; the function of the basic norm is to make it possible to consider this coercive order as an objectively valid order."

The system of norms, of law, has the *Grundnorm* as its foundation. Based upon this, the system of norms describes all legal meanings and provides all the rules of the law. Because each norm involves an official, and delimits their powers, the system as a whole authorises all officialdom. In so far as a state is a collection of persons holding official office, they are the product of norms, laws, and the state itself is the personification of the system of norms, laws. For Kelsen, there is no distinction between state and law – they are one and the same. It follows that there can be no opposition between state and law. The two concepts gaplessly overlap. Since officials are all equally authorised by the norms which create their roles, there is no distinction in Kelsen's system between different types of official. It follows that there is no basis for a separation of powers: legislature, executive and judiciary each comprise officials authorised by norms. It is only their functions which differ and the system as a whole is not concerned with matters of content.

Kelsen provides us with a compelling picture of a legal system. Political power is held by the state and is distributed from the constitution, through an organised system of inter-related norms into the hands of officials whose powers are both authorised and limited by the operation of those same norms. This is a powerful theory but it is not without difficulties. The *Grundnorm* presents a problem. Kelsen's initial intention is to do away with metaphysical entities. But the *Grundnorm* is a hypothetical postulate which is presupposed and upon which the entire system depends. It can hardly be described as an existent entity. It is fictitious and defies Kelsen's "scientific" analysis. Since the whole system of law depends upon the *Grundnorm* for validity, it would seem that in a revolution the whole constitution and system of law should cease to exist. But this is not necessarily what happens. Modern history shows us that legal systems may continue to have effect and what seems to be more important is whether the courts will continue to uphold the law. Kelsen's methodology is too rigid. Norms are said to have causal efficacy. This gives little room for the exercise of discretion, yet discretion is a prominent feature of our legal system. One has only to think of the discretionary way in which judges decide on sentencing – the wide range of factors to consider and disposals from which to choose in order to maximise social protection and minimise risk of reoffending. Kelsen's system describes the distribution of political power to officials. But it takes no account whatsoever of the content of the law. Form has prominence while meaning and content are ignored. Yet legal systems have to deal with issues of social concern and value such as persons and property. It is only their formal structure and activity which are explained. Kelsen relies on coercion as a necessary part of the analysis of the norm. Laws are obeyed primarily because of fear of sanctions. But in reality many laws do not refer to sanctions at all (for example, the laws which give power to people to make wills). Sanctions and unpleasant effects are not the same. Frequently there appears to be confusion between coercion and obligation.

HART'S *CONCEPT OF LAW*

While Hobbes, Austin and (indirectly) Kelsen took a "top down" view of political and legal power, Hart (1907–92) takes an opposing view. He says: "What is most needed, as a corrective to the model of coercive orders or rules, is a fresh conception of legislation as the introduction or modification of general standards of behaviour to be followed by the society generally." For Hart, laws are forms of social rule and their power and authority arise as social facts rooted in social behaviour, the behaviour of the people who comprise the society. Legal behaviour is a form of social behaviour and yet it differs from other forms of social behaviour in that it is obligatory. Hart says: "the most prominent general feature of law at all times and places is that its existence means that certain kinds of human conduct are no longer optional but in some sense obligatory" and he hopes to provide "an improved analysis of the distinctive structure of a municipal legal system and a better understanding of the resemblances and differences between law, coercion, and morality, as types of social phenomena".

It is no surprise that Hart starts by examining social behaviour which he divides into social habits and social rules. Social habits are customs or agreed forms of convergent behaviour; like a group of friends agreeing to go to the cinema every week. Failure by one of them to turn up one week would be a pity but not remarkable. However, social rules are different. Failure to adhere to a social rule would provide grounds for criticism by others in the social group and indeed self-criticism by the offender who is likely to feel a sense of guilt or shame. Laws are social rules, as are also the rules of morality and certain other forms of customary behaviour. It is not the rule-like character of law which gives it this force (for there are rules of games, rules of language and logic etc). The rule-ordered nature of laws shows that behaviour is convergent and regular. But the particular normative character of law and morality, as social rules, give rise to the use of the language of "right" and "wrong", "good" and "bad" and so on.

It follows that laws have two aspects: an external aspect and an internal aspect. The external aspect is the regularity and convergence of behaviour. If a Martian were to sit on a wall next to traffic lights, he would notice that people tended to stop their cars at red lights and to go at green. The Martian would be able to infer from this behaviour that a social rule was in existence. This is the external aspect. The Martian would not, however, know what it is like to conform to the rule nor would he know why the people obey it. We obey rules principally because we feel a social pressure to conform to them. We know that if we disobey the rule we will have to suffer the wrath and indignation of others in our society. Hart writes:

> "the external point of view, which limits itself to the observable regularities of behaviour, cannot reproduce ... the way in which the rules function ... in the lives of those who normally are the majority in society. ... For them the violation of the rule is not merely a basis for the prediction that a hostile reaction will follow but a reason for [that] hostility".

There are, of course, other reasons for compliance: we may fear the coercive force of the law, or we may rationally acknowledge that the law was enacted to fulfil the purposes achieving the common good. The feeling of a social pressure to conform to the law and hence to obey it is the internal aspect of a social rule. It is this which, more than any other motive, produces the efficacy of the law – that the majority of the people will obey it.

Nevertheless, laws have content. The content is in general decided by the political leaders. Laws are directions of general application and are addressed to all persons within the territory of the political power concerned. They differ from commands in that they are general. Laws are authoritative in that they are authorised through organised political processes and procedures. People are in the habit of voluntary obedience and so laws will usually have efficacy but in addition they are supported by the coercive power of the state in the event of non-compliance. Hart says:

> "there must, wherever there is a legal system, be some person or body of persons issuing general orders backed by threats which are generally obeyed, and it must be generally believed that these threats are likely to be implemented in the event of disobedience".

This person or body must be internally supreme and externally independent. If, following Austin, we call such a supreme and independent person or body of person the sovereign, the laws of any country will be the general orders backed by threats which are issued either by the sovereign or by subordinates in obedience to the sovereign. Nevertheless, not all laws are general orders. Some are power conferring. Hart gives the examples of "rules specifying what must be done to make wills, contracts or other arrangements which confer rights and create obligations". Not all laws therefore involve breaches of legal duties. In addition, the vertical structure of laws whereby the sovereign's power is imposed downwards is not necessarily reflected in the way laws come to be. Some, if not most, will be legislation enacted by a sovereign political authority, but others may arise as a matter of custom – as is the case with the common law which has existed and has been enforced by the courts from time immemorial.

Hart defines the legal system as "a union of primary and secondary rules". The primary rules are the general rules which regulate the behaviour of the public. A system of laws of that nature alone could survive in a relatively simply society. But in a complex society, particularly one which is sensitive to changes in the political and social environment, three particular problems or "defects" are encountered which necessitate three particular solutions for which Hart requires secondary rules. Each type of secondary rule is addressed to a particular type of official.

- First, there is the persistent question as to which laws to recognise. When is a law valid within the society? This is called the "**defect of uncertainty**". Hart answers this problem by proposing a secondary "rule of recognition". This rule states where and how are we to recognise a legal rule as existing and as valid and what is its proper scope. The officials who operate this rule will be the judiciary. In a similar way Hart is able to call upon rules of recognition to explain how one sovereign can succeed to another.

- Second, there is the "**defect of static rules**" which may occur when a set of rules is promulgated and thereafter must be followed indefinitely. Should laws really continue indefinitely? As a system of rules, laws will continue in full force and effect, but there may come a time when rules require to be repealed or amended and indeed new rules will be required if the society's legal system is not to stagnate. Hart's answer is that there must be "rules of change" whereby officials will create new rules or repeal or amend existing ones. These powers may be simple or complex; the powers conferred may be unrestricted or limited in various ways; or they may define the persons to legislate or the procedures to be followed. In each case the officials to who have the powers will be legislators. Given that the authority and values of the law come from the people who form the society, does this mean that legislators are reactive only rather than pro-active when law making?

- Third, it is well known that, while most people will obey the law, there are always some who do not. Hart calls this the "**defect of insufficiency of diffuse social pressure**". There therefore needs to be some system of enforcement. It is here that the coercive power of law should be felt. Hart's answer is that there must therefore be "rules of adjudication" whereby judges (and others) will enforce the law – by coercion if necessary. Judges are given the task of stating authoritatively whether a given rule has been broken and are mandated to enforce it or impose punishment. In addition to adjudication judges will generally also require to operate a rule of recognition since a prerequisite of determining the obligation is that the obligation is declared as a valid law in the first place.

Hart's form of social Positivism is sometimes called "modified Positivism". Law has imperative force. Laws are necessitated by our human nature. Hart describes law as having a "minimum content of natural law". This has five aspects (strongly reminiscent of Hobbes). First, all people are vulnerable. The law should set out to protect people who are vulnerable. Second, we are all approximately equal. Even the strong man is vulnerable at times and so will need protection at times. Third, we have limited altruism. We are all selfish some of the time and our selfish urges need to be curbed by power of law. Fourth, there are limited resources. The law is required to enable an equitable sharing of resources. This is reminiscent of Aristotle's distributive justice. Fifth, we are tempted to concern ourselves with our short-term interests but the law requires us to sacrifice these for communal long-term interests. The effects of these aspects of human nature are that the law must intervene to curb our nature and conform it to the common good. The law therefore performs tasks which are similar to those of morality. However, it must not be inferred that the law is simply imposing morality. It is just that its aims and those of morality have a tendency to approximate.

Hart notices that all forms of law involve rules and this includes statutes, case decisions, customary law, and international law. Rules operate to state what people must do in certain specified situations. Each rule specifies the situation and the persons affected. Rules are normative –they set the standard of behaviour to be followed in the specific situation. In addition, the rules are part of a system. But rules are generalisations which are given verbal expression. As forms of language, they may suffer from ambiguities, generalities, and problems of definitional obscurity. When a park byelaw says that no vehicles are allowed in the park, this clearly indicates a prohibition on cars and probably motorbikes. But does it prevent bicycles or skateboards? The word "vehicle" must be defined. Any general term produces "penumbra of uncertainty". As a result, systems of inter-related rules must have an open-texture. Specific circumstances are regulated but there are areas where the application of law is less certain. As a result, when a judge considers a case he uses his knowledge of the rule to decide what a party should have done to fulfil the demands of a rule or what the parties' behaviour should have been. In difficult cases the judge must decide the area of operation of the rule. He will look at the language used to state the rule, the context of the rule within the system as a whole, the purpose of the rule, and where relevant the judge will apply his knowledge of society's other standards, including moral standards, to decide whether the boundaries of the rule are to be extended or contracted to fit the persons and the facts about whom and which he is deciding. Thus a judge seeks to provide a proper interpretation (construction) and application of a rule in its specific factual context.

DWORKIN'S INTERPRETATIVE THEORY – LAW AS INTEGRITY

Ronald Dworkin takes a stance which is critical of Positivism. Law is not simply a system of rules. It is a system of rights and duties which depends upon underlying values which dictate the ways in which it should be interpreted. A descriptive view of law is not enough. Participation is required. Courts need to interpret sources of law (constitutions, statutes and precedents). In many cases the courts are able simply to apply a rule, but in "hard cases" the courts cannot simply apply rules. This is because a rule-ordered system of laws has an open texture – it is full of gaps and inconsistencies. Instead of starting the process of interpretation with the ways in which governments use coercive force, it is necessary to examine principles of interpretation laid out in advance within the law and legal practices. Courts require to consider community legal practices while at the same time respecting individual rights. These practices will involve moral, political and economic considerations. Not surprisingly, there is no settled view on which of these social factors should take priority and so it follows that there is a diversity in the ways in which the balance may be struck. Nevertheless the diversity approximates around what might be described as the "right" answer to a legal problem. This is illustrated in Dworkin's example of an omniscient judge, "Hercules", who is immensely wise and has a complete knowledge of the law and legal sources. Hercules would be able to produce the "right" answer which is the theory which best fits the law and sources as a whole. The law comprises rules and principles (and values, such as equality and liberty, which inform our fundamental rights). As a result, Dworkin clearly rejects the Positivist thesis that law depends on sources rather than merits. For him, the merits are essential, for the main function of a judge is to interpret and apply law justly.

MacCORMICK AND THE INSTITUTIONS OF LAW

MacCormick gives a descriptive analysis of law. A legal system is not an invention created in a vacuum. Laws are rooted in the usages and practices of human beings who have social co-existence. The system comprises a set of interrelated behavioural rules. Much of human social behaviour is rule ordered. Law is simply a special type of social behaviour. Our understanding of rules is learned through our experience in various areas of social interaction. There are four ways in particular that we learn that about rules. First, as language-using creatures, we are aware that rules and other conventions lie behind and provide the grammar and meaning of our language. If we did not comply with the conventions of language we simply could not communicate with one another. So we learn to use the rules of language even though we may not be consciously aware of them. Most of the time we would not even be able to express the rules of language. This is because the rules of language are not written down and are mere common understandings within a linguistic community. Second, we learn of rules through nurture, socialisation, and education. Here, we are taught the common views of "right" and "wrong" and we learn to comply with the commonly held view. Third, we meet rules in more institutionalised settings and in particular in general family and social relations. This includes the experience of school which has compulsory attendance and other rules. We also learn that rules are associated with religious observances and in sports and games. In these cases rules may be imposed by officials or representative bodies. Fourth, we see the more distant state agencies such as police and courts which impose rules in a more indirect way. The rules they impose are created by parliaments or other agencies and these rules are publicised to us by means of a written form.

Quite apart from their formal nature, rules also have content. The content arises from social behaviour and utility. MacCormick gives the example of queueing. We encounter the practice of queueing in waiting for a bus or taxi, waiting for security at airports, when buying stamps in a post office and in a whole range of other ways. Queueing is a generic practice with many variants. In most cases people will acknowledge that they are equals and will take their place in the queue along with others. Those who are at the head of the queue have priority, while those behind must wait their turn. There are some people who feel exalted and would wish to have priority over others. They may wish to jump the queue. Some of these may accept the existence of a queue to be a disagreeable part of the service that they require and so put up with the practice of queueing. Yet others may push their way to the head of the queue. There are therefore good reasons why the practice of queueing may become institutionalised in the interests of fairness. MacCormick gives the example of queueing in Waverley Station for information. Here, the practice of queueing is formalised. There is a numerical roll of tickets. One takes a ticket which has a number upon it and waits one's turn to be called for service. The practice is controlled. Two types of official are involved. There are "norm givers", persons who state what the rules are whereby the practice is to be controlled, and there are "norm implementers", persons who enforce the practice according to the rules. In the case of waiting for information at Waverley Station, the rules are enforced by the service personnel who will not serve anyone other than the person whose number has just been called. If a person fails to attend when their number is called, they lose their place in the queue. In this way the practice of queueing has become institutionalised. Law involves many such practices and not surprisingly also involves norm givers and norm implementers.

The law is a normative institutional order in the sense that there exist rules, harnessing social practices, which dictate how the practice will be conducted. The term "normative" means that the rule specifies the conditions whereby an action is "right" or "wrong". MacCormick continues his analysis by insisting that every rule specifies a set of "operative facts". Where these facts occur, the rule operates and produces a "normative consequence". Wrong actions are prohibited by the norm implementers, while right actions are endorsed by them. In the case of laws, the norm givers are usually legislators. The norm implementers are enforcing officials and so may be judges. The function of enforcing officials is to supervise and monitor the practice which is rule ordered. The function of judges is to make formal decisions and forms of appeal.

Rules may be applied strictly or with discretion. A strict application of rules requires that wherever the operative facts occur they have one fixed normative consequence. In a discretionary application of rules, the rule follower is expected to consider the full facts and circumstances and then decide within a range of alternatives in accordance with some form of equitable interpretation. Standards may be brought into account. A "seasonable" action is one where a person has a level of latitude as to when to carry out an action they are free to do. A "reasonable" action is one where a person has a latitude as to the different forms of action which they may carry out.

The norm givers and norm implementers are officials of the state. The state gives the rules legal authority and its functions are divisible into legislature (norm givers), executive (as enforcing norm implementers), and judiciary (as norm-implementing decision-makers and interpreters). Thus, the state can be seen to be divided into separate powers (the "Separation of Powers"). But the state's authority is limited by its being territorial (it has effective political control only over a specific territory), legitimate (in the sense that it must be recognised by citizens as having exclusive authority within the territory) and independent (in the sense that it must be free from any external interference by any other authority).

Every state has a constitution which creates legal institutions and provides for the formalisation and articulation of rules which the citizens will then use to guide their decisions and conduct. In every case there will be state officials who will observe and uphold the constitution and the laws validly made under it. The observance of the laws by officials and citizens is essential to any efficacious law-state.

All rule-ordered systems of law encounter difficulties of application and interpretation. The legislature must not impose laws which depart materially from what people actually do. This is because laws are based upon well-established forms of social behaviour. The efficacy of the law depends upon the legislators' ability to harness these forms of behaviour for the intended ends of the law. If a gap between the law and actual social practices is created, this will cause people to fail to behave in the way expected of them. This could be described as an "efficiency gap".

Having described how a system of normative institutional order can exist and operate, MacCormick passes to the purposes for which law is intended. These purposes include protecting certain social values. The first of these values is given over to identifying persons as centres of autonomous choice and action. People are capable of obeying or disobeying laws, of doing their duty or failing to do their duty. Strictly speaking, people have to choose between doing a "wrong" action or a "not-wrong" action. When people commit wrongs they are said to be legally responsible for their actions. Rules should clearly express the duties which people are under. People should know what their duty is when the operative facts occur. MacCormick says they should learn that it is wrong to omit to *v*, when *v*-ing is obligatory, and vice versa. We describe this usage using the term "obligation" and this commonly goes hand in hand with the broad use of the term "duty". This is reinforced by the normative language of "right" and "wrong".

It is a primary duty on individual persons not to harm others and on this depends the operation of the criminal law.

Out of the concept of persons (and the concepts of duties and obligations) arises the idea of rights (which we shall look at in Chapter 8).

Another important concept is the idea of property. MacCormick says that property in all its forms is norm-dependent. But it is a matter of the state's choice as to what kinds of property any particular legal system will recognise. Ultimately, the choice is a question of politics, guided by economics and perhaps moral philosophy. In many cases property rights will be held by individuals, but it is quite conceivable that they may be held by the public in general. In this way full socialisation of property is possible and in that event the law will stipulate how particular things may actually be used by particular persons. Ownership is defined as the recognition of property over which particular powers are devolved on to particular individuals or groups of individuals.

The rights and powers of the state are not themselves without legal control. Constraints on the state's powers will be imposed to protect the fundamental rights and liberties of individuals. Laws must be aimed towards achieving the common good whereby the state sets out to promote private life, commerce and the autonomy of individuals. In doing this a balance requires to be set. MacCormick writes:

> "The institutional character of law is intelligible only on an assumption concerning the intrinsic ends of the enterprise of governance under law: these are the realisation of justice and the common good, according to some reasonable conception of these ... One has to consider the differing but complementary values implicit in these legal domains: orderly government and distributive justice; civil peace and distributive justice; private life and market economies; [all] underpinned by remedial measures of corrective justice. ... human artefacts and contrivances, including any rules which people try to live or get others to live [by], have to be understood functionally. What is their point, what is the final cause to which they are orientated? They perform well or ill, are in good shape or bad, to the extent that they can be seen to work towards these essential ends with the minimum of regrettable side effects. It is undoubtedly controversial what functions should be ascribed to law in general or to particular laws or any other human production."

MacCORMICK ON SOVEREIGNTY

The connection between political power, law and morality

MacCormick says that there is a distinction to be made between the state's system of political power and principles of law and morality. There are four possible types of state which can therefore come about:

- The state may be law dependent, as is the case under a theory of Natural Law. On such a view, law is a type of the rational norms of conduct which are built into the nature of things and of people and thereby bring about intrinsic rationality and goodness. The state law will conform to Natural Law and so will conform to reason and morality. In such a system the government is charged with upholding the rights of all citizens.

- The law may be state dependent. The state and its institutions will be legitimate only where they uphold and give adequate form to law and to rights derived from that law. Clearly, some form of Social Contract is the background to this kind of state. Rulers and sovereigns will be entitled to hold power only as long as their rule is effective and provides the people with a sufficiency of rights and advantages. This will cause the people to provide their continuing consent.

- The state and the law may be separate but co-existent. The state has complete monopoly over the law and morality. Government power will be centralised and the law is the means by which behaviour within the society will be controlled and influenced. This view contradicts MacCormick's idea of law as normative institutionalised order since law should be rooted in the usages and practices of the society. This means acknowledging the values of the people rather than politically overruling them. This sort of state will suffer from weaknesses when the political policy varies from the usages and practices of social co-existence.

- There is an identity of state and law. MacCormick favours this view, saying that the identity of state and law is imperfect in the case of the United Kingdom. This type of state should not merely create laws but will do other things as well, such as controlling armies, running health services, providing systems of agricultural subsidies etc. The law and the state will be aimed at providing the common good.

Sovereign state or post-sovereign state?

In the United Kingdom the political state is to be identified with the Westminster Parliament. However, the accession of the United Kingdom to the European Union in 1972 questions this. On one view, rejected by MacCormick, there was a quiet revolution since the traditional sovereignty of the Queen in Parliament had been overturned and powers seceded to the European Union as a new super-state. MacCormick disagrees and says that this event created a new legal order *sui generis*. A further level was created by devolution of Westminster powers to the Scottish Parliament in 1998. MacCormick says that as a result of these constitutional law changes, the power of the state has been reconfigured and that there now exists a multi-layered governmental system. Some functions are now controlled by the European Union which may make rules and whose courts may make decisions with direct effect in the United Kingdom. Other functions are performed by the devolved governments. The ultimate power of government is divided and people therefore look to and give obedience to different governmental authorities. MacCormick says that this is not without precedent, for in previous ages people gave obedience to the different authorities of Emperor and Pope. However, any such multi-layered governmental system can survive only if they all pursue the same values and goals.

As a result, Austin's idea of the sovereign state having complete and undivided power over the subjects is now a historical anomaly. It may have been important for 200 years, but it is now a thing of the past. Our times may best be characterised as times of "post-sovereignty". There are several ways of explaining this. The "diffusionist" view says that governmental powers may diffuse upwards to the organs of the European Union, and downwards to the component countries of the United Kingdom and perhaps to the regions as well. The alternative view is the "sovereigntist" view whereby the United Kingdom Parliament is still the source of all sovereignty and it is simply a matter of policy to let the European Union and the devolved administrations use some of the powers. On the sovereigntist view the United Kingdom Government retains the power to withdraw from the European Union. The sovereigntist view is still be held quite strongly in some quarters. MacCormick is clearly in the diffusionist camp. This is because he holds a social democratic view of authority: "It is to the people as a whole that belongs the decision about the exact specification of [constitutionally derivative] rights, and about the other elements of constitutional structure and the distribution of constitutional authority." Since the people have voted for these major constitutional changes, it follows that a multi-layered governmental system does indeed exist.

MacCormick says that we should also consider our theories of law. Sovereignty involves concentrations of power in the hands of different groups or communities. The existence of the European Union suggests that there is sovereignty, legitimated by the electorate across the whole of Europe, which may dictate rules common to the European Union as a territory. At the same time, at more local levels, there is a need for smaller groups to assert their views on more local issues. This gives rise to the concept of subsidiarity. Decisions should be taken at the most local level if they can be. But at the wider level there may be great agreement on human rights and other rights of wider community concern such as civil and political, and perhaps also economic and social rights. Where political rights are affected, our ideas of democracy may have to change accordingly.

One feature of subsidiarity is that it gives scope to the phenomenon of nationalism. MacCormick predicts the division of the United Kingdom into two or more successor states, all of which will have representation and voting rights in the various organs of the European Union. All this would require negotiation at the United Kingdom level as well as at local and European levels. This would necessitate what were previously United Kingdom responsibilities being reviewed and partitioned equitably. Public utilities would require to be re-organised on an appropriate basis. Vital ministries of state would have to be divided and a separate form created for Scotland (to include social security, trade and industry, treasury, defence and foreign affairs). If MacCormick is correct in his prediction, radical changes in United Kingdom governmental structures and institutions are to be expected.

MacCORMICK ON JUDICIAL DECISION-MAKING

MacCormick provides an interesting and authoritative descriptive view of judicial decision-making. The view is also normative since it shows how judicial decision-making should be carried out.

Syllogistic logic and deduction

Judges behave in logical ways and express their judgments in terms of rules and logic. The logical form of this reasoning is that of the syllogism. An example of the syllogism is:

> Major premise: All men are mortal;
> Minor premise: Socrates is a man;
> Conclusion: Therefore: Socrates is mortal.

The conclusion necessarily follows from valid premises.

In some cases ("easy" cases) given the operative facts, a rule can be applied strictly and the normative outcome is logically deduced. MacCormick in *Legal Reasoning and Legal Theory* gives the example of the case of *Daniels and Daniels* v *R White and Sons and Tabard* (1938). Mr Daniels went into a pub and bought a bottle of lemonade which turned out to be contaminated with carbolic acid. The Sale of Goods Act 1893, s 14 requires that goods shall be of merchantable quality. Mr Daniels was entitled to recover damages. The conclusion was derived logically from the facts, given the rule. A deductive argument is valid if, whatever may be the content of the premises and the conclusion, its form is such that its premises imply or entail the conclusion.

Nor is it only judges who use syllogistic logic. The pleadings of the parties to any case will present their arguments in a syllogistic form. They submit to the court that, given the operative facts, the law favours their client. The contest between parties is expressed by both sides as opposing syllogisms. But not all cases can be decided this way.

Indeterminacy of rules

In *Rhetoric and the Rule of Law* MacCormick gives a number of ways in which rules may be indeterminate. Legal rules are expressed in natural language and "these are afflicted with ambiguity, vagueness and open texture". Ambiguity may come about as a result of the use of terms, concepts, standards and values, all of which require definition. Discretion may introduce vagueness. Open texture in particular causes "hard" cases which may come about where the facts do not fit within the strict expression of a legal rule. The law is "gappy". In these "hard" cases the legal rules need to be interpreted. In addition, the deductive method does not always provide just results. In many cases there is a need to avoid the application of strict justice. In the idea of equity the merits of an individual case may be brought into account in order to provide a just result.

Development of rules and Interpretation

In *Legal Reasoning and Legal Theory*, MacCormick analyses the problem of applying rules to facts into three steps which allow the rules to develop:

- First, there are problems of "relevancy" which ask what valid legal rules should be applied to the problem. There may be a gap in the law which may introduce a conflict between different rules.

- Second, there are problems of "interpretation" which ask how legal rules should be interpreted – stretched to fit the operative facts. Where a gap exists, rules often require interpretation in this way. This may mean looking at the purposes for which rules have originally been made.

- Third, there are problems of "classification" which ask whether the facts of the case can be distinguished so as to bring them within the ambit of a recognised exception or other acknowledged set of circumstances for special treatment.

In *Rhetoric and the Rule of Law* MacCormick expands his ideas about interpretative arguments. There are three different categories, all of which depend on a legal rule being a general statement intended to have universal application. First, "linguistic" arguments, which look at the ordinary meaning of words where this is indicated as important, though this is sometimes contrasted with the technical meaning of expressions in specialist subject areas. In the main the ordinary or plain meanings of words should be pursued unless there are good reasons to the contrary. Second, there are six types of "systemic" arguments, which set out to harmonise the interpretation with the body of law in which the rule arises. These involve: (1) contextual harmonising the operation of the rule with its context; (2) arguing from precedents to harmonise the operation of the rule in particular sets of circumstances with the values which are espoused in previous cases; (3) extending a term's ordinary use by means of analogy from similar expressions in the surrounding law; (4) conceptual arguments which favour conceptual uniformity within particular areas of law; (5) arguing from general principles so that sub-principles are ranked in order of importance; and (6) arguments from history which prefer a traditional form of interpretation to novel or unusual forms. Third, there are "teleologic-evaluative" arguments which note that rules of law or statutes are aimed by legislators towards specific ends or the preservation of particular values and should be interpreted to give effect to their ends or to preserve their values.

Second-order reasoning

Judging is a form of practical reasoning and in cases where no clear or just deductive ruling can be made, it is necessary for the judge to consider making a "second-order" ruling – the logic is second order as secondary results of a rule's application may have to be assessed in practice in order to ascertain how the rule is to be applied. There are three forms of second-order reasoning:

- "Consequentialist" arguments which consider the balance of costs and benefits of different interpretations of the rule and seek the most just consequences.

- "Evaluative" rulings which are designed to make the best use of values implicit in the law. "The fundamental precepts of law according to high but ancient authority are these three: live honestly, harm nobody, treat all persons with the respect due to them." Areas of law may support different values. In delict the integrity of persons has priority. In contract the liberty of persons to pursue their own ends, balanced against fidelity to undertakings and mutual trust and good faith, are the priority. In criminal law public peace and order and personal security and integrity are the operative values. In trust law the operative value is fidelity. In each case the consequences of operating a rule should be evaluated by giving the values inherent in the rule their proper place.

- "Subjective" judgments are those whereby judges will evaluate the different terms and concepts they use to make their decisions. "Reasonableness" is a concept which raises such issues. Judges will take into account the degree of perceived injustice, or predicted inconvenience that may arise. Principles of justice, analogies, extrapolations, and modifications will require to be balanced in order to reach an appropriate coherence of competing values.

Judicial conservatism

Statutes and rules of precedent have to be properly interpreted so that the judge does not depart from common-sense meanings of words or from the values which statutes promote. Previous cases should not be departed from without good reasons. The same applies to accepted understandings of policy and principle which have been used to support previous decisions. Sources of law must be interpreted in a way that is understandable by the public (so that the public may use them as a guide to future action). The final decision should not offend traditional conceptions of justice and common sense. All decisions must be "universalisable". They must not be *ad hoc* or *ad hominem* – there must be no individual interpretations. In every case a rule or a principle or indeed a policy should provide a universalised or generic ruling in terms of its effects.

While MacCormick's analysis of judicial decision-making is complex (and has varied over his period of philosophical flourishing) the essence of his views is that the syllogistic form is of prime importance and in general should be used wherever possible. Where it cannot, it will become necessary to analyse the problem which prevents its use. Outcomes of different alternatives need to be weighed up and balanced. A variety of techniques may be used but the final decision should reflect generally held values within the judicial community and within the law itself. Judicial conservatism will usually be followed, but in all cases the decision should be seen as an instance of a universalised rule rather than an *ad hoc* decision. Like cases have to be treated alike while departures from previous decisions must be grounded in the operative facts and relevant factors that occur.

Essential concepts

- Legal Positivism takes the view that the validity of law depends on its sources and not its merits. While not denying that morality may have a place, Positivists deny that there is any necessary connection between law and morality.

Austin

- Austin defined a law as the command of a sovereign. There are three essential elements to a law as a command: (1) sovereign, (2) subject and (3) sanction.

Kelsen

- Kelsen sets out to produce a pure science of law. He strips away all extraneous and not strictly legal material which includes any sociological, psychological or political elements. These obscure the essence of the law.

- Once cleansed, law contains norms (rules which say what ought to happen). Laws primarily set a standard of behaviour which people should follow. The formula for this is: if X then Y, if not-Y then Z (if circumstances X occur, then do action Y; and if action Y is not done, then the appointed official should do action Z). People should obey the law but if they don't then an official is under a duty to impose a sanction.

- A legal system has continuing legitimacy because it has effectiveness in the sense that the system is accepted by a majority of citizens and, even if it is disobeyed, the official who must impose the sanction will accept the duties the law creates. Individual norms may cease to have effectiveness when they cease to be accepted by the majority of citizens and officials no longer impose them. This gives rise to the phenomenon of desuetude.

- Norms are rooted in social contexts which they address. The norms provide a legal meaning. The persons under obligation, either public or official, understand the legal meanings in the context which the norm addresses. Every situation has an external and an internal view. On the external view, there is an action, a piece of behaviour. The internal view provides the meaning which is subjectively understood by the participants.

- Norms either arise through custom or are enacted by conscious legislative acts.

- The validity of the legal system is provided by the *Grundnorm*, or basic norm. It is unquestioned by the members of the society and is the ultimate source of political power and of the authority of the state. The *Grundnorm* is not expressed and has no content. It is presupposed.

- For Kelsen, there is no distinction between state and law – they are one and the same. Since all officials are authorised by the norms which create their roles, there is no distinction in Kelsen's system between different types of official. There is no basis for a separation of powers among legislature, executive and judiciary. It is only their functions which differ.

- Political power is held by the state, is distributed from the constitution, through an organised system of inter-related norms into the hands of officials whose powers are both authorised and limited by the operation of those same norms.

Hart

- For Hart, laws are forms of social rule and their power and authority arise as social facts rooted in social behaviour, the behaviour of the people who comprise the society.

- Hart makes a distinction between social habits and social rules. Social habits are customs or agreed forms of convergent behaviour but failure to follow the pattern has no adverse consequences. Social rules are obligatory. Failure to follow a social rule provides grounds for criticism by others and self-criticism and produces a sense of guilt or shame. Laws and moral rules are both types of social rules.

- Laws have an external aspect and an internal aspect. The external aspect is the regularity and convergence of behaviour. The internal aspect is the feeling of social pressure to conform to the rule.

- Laws have content which is in general decided by the political leaders but some laws arise through custom. Laws are authoritative directions of general application and are addressed to all persons within the territory of the political power concerned. People are in the habit of voluntary obedience.

- Hart defines the legal system as "a union of primary and secondary rules". The primary rules are the general rules which regulate the behaviour of the public. A complex legal system encounters three particular problems or "defects" which necessitate three particular solutions for which Hart requires secondary rules addressed to officials. First, the there is the "defect of uncertainty" which is that people do not always know what valid laws apply. This is solved by the "rule of recognition" whereby a judge states which valid legal rules apply and state what their proper scope is. Second, there is the "defect of static rules" which indicates that laws which are to be followed indefinitely would lead to a stagnation of the law. This is answered by "rules of change" whereby officials can create new rules or repeal or amend existing ones. Third, there is the "defect of insufficiency of diffuse social pressure" which arises because people may not always obey the laws. This is answered by "rules of adjudication" whereby judges (and others) will enforce the law – by coercion if necessary.

- Hart's form of Social Positivism is sometimes called "Modified Positivism". Laws have imperative force but they are related to our human needs which Hart describes as their having a "minimum content of Natural Law". This has five aspects. First, all people are vulnerable and the law should protect the vulnerable. Second, we are all approximately equal. Third, we have limited altruism and may have to be forced to co-operate with others. Fourth, there are limited resources which need to be shared equitably. Fifth, we are tempted to concern ourselves with our short-term interests but the law requires us to sacrifice these for communal long-term interests. The law forces us to conform to the common good.

- All forms of law involve rules and this includes statutes, case decisions, customary law and international law. Each rule specifies the situation and the persons affected. Where laws use a general term this can produce "penumbra of uncertainty". A system of inter-related rules will have an open-texture. In difficult cases a judge must decide the area of operation of the rule. The judge will seek to provide a proper interpretation (construction) and application of a rule in its specific factual context.

Dworkin

- Dworkin is critical of Positivism. Law is not simply a system of rules. There are underlying values which dictate the ways in which a rule should be interpreted. In "hard cases" the courts must consider community legal practices while at the same time respecting individual rights. These practices will involve moral, political and economic considerations laid out in advance.

- Dworkin gives the example of an omniscient judge, "Hercules", who is immensely wise and has a complete knowledge of the law and legal sources and in particular the rules and principles of interpretation. Hercules would be able to produce the "right" answer, which is the theory which best fits the law and sources as a whole.

MacCormick

- MacCormick says that laws are rooted in the usages and practices of human beings who have social co-existence. Law is simply a special type of rule-ordered social behaviour.

- Our understanding of rules is learned through our experience in various areas of social interaction such as our use of language; our experience of nurture, socialisation and education; our experience of institutionalised settings; and the more distant state agencies such as police and courts.

- The content arises from social behaviour and utility. MacCormick gives the example of queueing.

- Institutionalised normative order involves officially controlled practices. There are "norm givers", persons who state what the rules are whereby the practice is to be controlled, and there are "norm implementers", persons who enforce the practice according to the rules. In the case of law, norm givers are generally legislators. Norm implementers are enforcing officials and judges.

- "Normative" indicates that the rule specifies the conditions whereby an action is "right" or "wrong".

- Rules may be applied strictly or with discretion. A strict application of rules requires that wherever the operative facts occur they have one fixed normative consequence. In a discretionary application of rules, the rule follower is expected to consider the full facts and circumstances and then decide within a range of alternatives in accordance with some form of equitable interpretation.

- In every case there will be state officials who will observe and uphold the constitution and the laws validly made under it. The observance of the laws by officials and citizens is essential to any efficacious law-state.

- All rule-ordered systems of law encounter difficulties of application and interpretation. The legislature must not impose laws which depart materially from what people actually do. This is because laws are based upon well-established forms of social behaviour.

- Law protects social values.

- Persons are centres of autonomous choice and action. People are capable of obeying or disobeying laws, of doing their duty or failing to do their duty. People are legally responsible for their actions. Rules should clearly express the duties which people are under. People have rights.

- Property is norm dependent. But it is a matter of the state's choice as to what kinds of property any particular legal system will recognise. Ultimately, the choice is a question of politics, guided by economics and perhaps moral philosophy. Property may be held by individuals or by the public in general. "Ownership" is defined as the recognition of property over which particular powers are devolved on to particular individuals or groups of individuals.

- The rights and powers of the state are legally controlled. The fundamental rights and liberties of individuals should be protected. Laws must be aimed towards achieving the common good. In doing this a balance requires to be struck.

- MacCormick says there is a distinction to be made between the state's system of political power and principles of law and morality. There are four forms. First, state may be law dependent, as is the case under a theory of Natural Law. Second, the law may be state dependent. Third, the state and law may be separate but co-existent. Fourth, there is an identity of state and law. MacCormick favours this view, saying that the identity of state and law is imperfect in the case of the United Kingdom.

- The accession of the United Kingdom to the European Union in 1972 and the creation of the Scottish Parliament in 1998 questioned traditional sovereignty. MacCormick says that as a result of these constitutional law changes, there now exists a multi-layered governmental system. The ultimate power of government is divided and people therefore look to and give obedience to different governmental authorities.

- The "diffusionist" view says that governmental powers may diffuse upwards to the organs of the European Union, and downwards to the component countries of the United Kingdom.

- The "sovereigntist" view says that the United Kingdom Government retains the power to withdraw from the European Union. This preserves the traditional view of sovereignty as far as possible.

- MacCormick says that authority derives from democracy. The people have voted for constitutional changes, thus creating a multi-layered governmental system.

- On the wider scale, a multi-layered governmental system is possible because there are commonly held values.

- Decisions should be taken at the most local level if they can be. This is the principle of subsidiarity.

- A consequence of subsidiarity is nationalism.

- MacCormick predicts the division of the United Kingdom into two or more successor states, all of which will have representation and voting rights in the European Union. But this would also have major consequences for the present functions of the United Kingdom Government.

- In easy cases a rule can be applied strictly and the outcome is logically deduced. The syllogism is the exemplar of the relevant logic. The conclusion necessarily follows from valid premises.

- Where the deductive method does not provide the most just result, judges need to consider the reasons for this. Sometimes, equity may need to be brought into account.

- There are three types of problems in applying rules: problems of "relevancy," problems of "interpretation," and problems of "classification".

- Judges may have to consider "second order" rulings. There are "consequentialist" arguments, "evaluative" arguments and "subjective" arguments.

- Issues of interpretation of the operative rules are important. There are "linguistic" interpretations, "systemic" interpretations and "teleologic-evaluative" interpretations.

- Judges are conservatism in their decision-making. They should not depart from previous decisions without good reasons. They should be faithful to accepted understandings of policy and principle. They must ensure that sources of law are interpreted in a way that is understandable by the public.

- All decisions must be "universalisable". They should not be *ad hoc* or *ad hominem*. A rule, principle or policy should provide a universalised or generic ruling in terms of its effects and thereby preserve accepted values.

5 AMERICAN AND SCANDINAVIAN REALISM

There are two forms of "Realist" theories of law: the American and the Scandinavian Realists. They have very little in common. Both react against the idea of law as a set of axioms, rules and forms. Instead, they both seek to find a hidden reality in the law which has lain obscured by these axioms, rules and forms. Law is truly revealed when law is in action: when laws are obeyed, claims asserted, or courts resolve disputes. These behavioural aspects are the reality of law and not the axioms and rules of textbooks. But there the similarities end. American Realism looks principally at the processes of judicial decision-making, seeks to develop a science of law in action based on courts and judicial behaviour and seeks predictability of decisions as a goal. Scandinavian Realism, on the other hand, looks at the underlying psychological, social or economic motivations whereby we come to feel a sense of obligation under the law and regard the law as authoritative and binding. Of these, the psychological is the most important and explains the underlying feelings which cause people to obey law and follow its demands.

AMERICAN REALISM

Holmes and Rule Scepticism

The founder of the American Realist school was Oliver Wendell Holmes, a constitutional Supreme Court judge for 30 years. Holmes reacted against Formalism: the idea that the law is a set of rigid legal rules which merely have to be applied to the facts of a case. The apparent certainty of the law about which one reads in textbooks is a mere illusion. In textbooks, the logic of the law is often likened to a logical syllogism where one rule leads necessarily on to the next and finally to a foregone conclusion. All appears certain. But the application of rules in the courts is usually far from certain. Legal rules have general application (for the legislator thinks only in general terms) while the judge looks at particular factual circumstances which come before him. So, the judge needs first to interpret the rules and second to apply them pragmatically to the facts of the case. Holmes's rejection of the restrictive logic of rules is sometimes referred to as "Rule Scepticism". In Holmes's view, true law is judge made, not legislator made. True law exists only when the judge determines a case. Some idea of justice will be in the judge's mind. An actual judicial decision may therefore involve a judge considering moral, political and social principles, and indeed may include the particular prejudices which the judge shares with the common man and woman. This has the effect that in any court case, the way the judge will interpret and apply the rules to the facts will be far from clear, and the outcome of the case is quite unpredictable until the decision is made. It follows that the body of case law which is built up over time is far more real than the textbooks, statutes and principles. This is because judge–made precedent is a record of legal rules interpreted by judicial principles and applied to actual factual situations.

Holmes illustrates his point about unpredictability by referring to the "bad man" who simply wants to know what the outcome of the case will be for him and is not in the slightest interested in textbook legal argumentation. Holmes says:

> "take the fundamental question what constitutes the law? You will find some text writers telling you that it is something different from what is decided by the courts of Massachusetts or England, that it is a system of reason, that it is a deduction from principles of ethics or admitted axioms or what not, which may or may not coincide with the decisions. But if we take the view of our friend the bad man we shall find that he does not care two straws for the axioms or deductions, but that he does want to know what the Massachusetts or English courts are likely to do in fact. I am inclined to agree with him. The prophecies of what the courts will do in fact, and nothing more pretentious, are what I mean by the law. Take again a notion which as popularly understood is the widest conception which law contains; the notion of legal duty ... we fill the word with all the content which we draw from morals. But what does it mean to a bad man? Mainly, and in the first place, a prophecy that if he does certain things he will be subject to disagreeable consequences by way of imprisonment or compulsory payment of money".

Holmes concludes that a major, if not the major, difficulty in predicting the outcome of any particular case is to be found in the way that judges interpret and apply or even overrule the textbook rules (in the American system the Supreme Court judges can rule a statute contrary to the constitution and thus completely inoperative). A rigid system of rules has huge amounts of uncertainty about it (we may remember Hart's similar view about the "open texture" of rules). To resolve these difficulties, judges draw upon their experience of justice. Holmes says:

> "the life of the law has not been logic, it has been experience. The felt necessities of the time, the prevalent moral and political theories, intuitions of

public policy, avowed or unconscious, even the prejudices which judges share with their fellow men, have had a good deal more to do than the syllogism in determining the rules by which men should be governed".

Frank and Fact Scepticism

Jerome Frank reacted against Holmes's idea of Rule Scepticism. He thought that Holmes's viewpoint was narrow due to the fact that he was a judge operating an appellate jurisdiction. An appeal is concerned with the application of legal principles to a set of certain facts. The facts will have been found by the lower, trial, court after the hearing of witnesses. The lower court will determine what the facts are and will report those facts to the appellate court as "findings-in-fact". The appellate court must accept the facts as found by the lower court. This is to be expected since the appellate court has not heard the evidence and has no basis for assessing the issues of credibility and reliability of witnesses. Hence, it is Frank's view that, in an appeal, the only area where there remains any doubt is restricted to the interpretation and application of the rules. But what was far more important than any uncertainty about the meaning and application of legal rules is the selection of facts which the lower, trial, court finds proved. In Frank's view, fact-finding is the most difficult and influential part of the judicial decision-making. This is done when the judge or jury hears the evidence and makes the crucial decisions about what facts are held and which facts are rejected. Very often, once the facts have been construed by the lower court, the application of the legal principles is easy and obvious. In terms of the number of cases which are resolved by courts, most of them are resolved at the trial court level and relatively few go on to appellate courts as appeals. Frank proposes that any difficulties in predicting the outcome of cases is more likely to be produced by the assessment of the facts than the application of the rules. This stance is referred to as "Fact Scepticism". Frank explains this as follows:

> "Rules (whether made by legislatures or judge-made) are embodiments of social policies, values, ideals, and ... for that reason ... should be recurrently and informedly re-examined. ... But the rules, statutory or judge-made, are not self-operative. They are frustrated, inoperative, whenever, due to the faulty fact-finding in trial courts, they are applied to non-existent facts."

And elsewhere:

> "Generally most of the rule sceptics, restricting themselves to the upper-court level, live in an artificial two-dimensional legal world, while the legal world

of the fact-sceptics is three-dimensional. Obviously, many events occurring in the fact-sceptics" three-dimensional cosmos are out of sight, and therefore out of mind, in the rule-sceptics' cosmos."

In other words, during a trial, the fact finder (whether judge or jury) will hear a great deal of evidence, including conflicting evidence. The fact finders are therefore obliged to make up their minds as to what facts to accept and what to reject. They bring to their decision-making on the facts all their own prejudices and beliefs which colour the way they look at and judge the witnesses and hence the evidence. Sometimes these prejudices are obvious – they may depend upon racial, religious, economic or political factors, but there are many other factors too which are not so obvious. Frank suggests that a judge's class, education, and religion will be factors of importance. Hence the chief difficulty in finding predictability of the outcome of a case is "the inability, thanks to these inscrutable factors, to foresee what a particular trial judge or jury will believe to be the facts".

So, both Rule Sceptics and Fact Sceptics are pessimistic about the possibility of predicting the outcome of court decisions – but for different reasons. The true picture is that the bar to the prediction of the outcome of a case will involve both forms of scepticism. Is it possible to improve predictability?

Llewellyn

Karl Llewellyn was an important contributor to the idea of predictability. His stance is that of a Rule Sceptic but he also realised that resolving disputes was only one of the tasks that law performs. A system of laws provides society with the tools that it needs in a changing world, assuring the survival of the members and the maintenance of order and justice. Llewellyn identified a number of "law jobs": dealing with "trouble cases" and restoring order (Llewellyn likened this to "garage repair work"); channelling conduct and expectations so as to avoid trouble and to allow people to adjust to social change; providing members of society with integration, direction and incentive; providing authority and authoritative procedures; and creating judicial methods aimed at the settlement of disputes.

With regard to the resolution of disputes, judges oscillate between two different styles. Some judges may restrict themselves to a "formal" style, sticking rigidly to rules and applying them logically. Injustice may result. Far better is the "grand" style, where judges apply a "situation sense" and look at the purposes of the rules and other policy considerations and attempt to do justice. In the "grand" style, the judge draws upon professional and cultural ideals generally held within the legal profession and society, thus ensuring that there is much more stability in judicial decision-making than we might otherwise expect. Llewellyn says that these involve "ideology and a body of persuasive and powerful ideas which are largely unspoken, largely implicit, and which pass unmentioned in the books".

Schubert and Loevinger: judicial behaviour and *Jurimetrics*

Both Glendon Schubert and Lee Loevinger were concerned with researching and proposing ways in which legal decision-making could be made more predictable.

Schubert concerned himself with analysing scientifically a judge's background, temperament, economic status and attitudes towards specific social issues. In this way he believed that it should be possible to predict how the judge would make decisions in future cases. In *Judicial analysis and voting behaviour* (1963), Schubert used his analyses of specific judges' attitudes to show why they chose to make decisions in prominent legal cases as they did.

In the same year, Loevinger, in *Jurimetrics, the methodology of legal inquiry,* applied mathematical techniques to the analysis of legal decision-making systems. He did not concentrate upon individual judges. Instead, he regarded a court as an open system interacting with its environment and consisting of inter-related parts. The personnel of a court (judge, counsel, defendant, jury) all have their part to play as do the various interrelated rules and procedures. Decision-making therefore involves a large set of complex factors. Each factor has a determinate job to do. Any activity within part of the whole system will affect the other parts. A failure in one part of the system will have detrimental effects on the other parts and thereby on the outcome of the decision. Only by understanding the system fully will it be possible to take steps to improve predictability. These ideas have been used to develop improved practices and procedures. One example of this is the procedure of jury selection in the United States. In most countries, including Scotland, prosecution and defence may object to a particular juror on justifiable grounds. In Scotland such objection is extremely rare. However, the United States allows in-depth examination of jurors either collectively or individually. While such juror selection is designed to produce an impartial jury and thus a verdict with greater authority, it has been suggested by some that at times jurors may be chosen in order to produce a particular bias.

In practice it is difficult to do analyses of judge and jury decision-making. Advances in computer techniques have offered the hope that complicated models can be developed. Recent advances in artificial intelligence (AI), in chaos theory, game theory and fuzzy logic have been applied to legal issues with some success.

SCANDINAVIAN REALISM

The Scandinavian Realists also reacted against formalism. They, like Kelsen, wished to remove all meaningless metaphysical elements from law and hoped to find the underlying reality rooted in the fundamental facts of existence – where, how and why we carry out acts with legal significance. This purism meant that they rejected concepts of good, bad and just. The Scandinavian Realists were particularly interested in the concepts of rights and obligations provided they could rescue them from metaphysical obscurity. Unlike the American Realists, the Scandinavian Realists were not primarily lawyers but were conceptual thinkers rooted in empiricism. The result of their thinking emphasises the importance of psychological, social and economic motivations.

Hägerström

Axel Hägerström disliked the idea of legal rules and formed the view that to a great extent the language of law is nothing but illusion. In order to find the underlying facts within the concepts of rights, duties, obligation, property, justice and so on, he examined the legal concepts using a methodology that he likened to an onion. Just as an onion is made up of layer upon layer, so he hoped to strip metaphysical elements away from legal concepts in order to find the inner factual content. His analysis of rights illustrates this. "Having a right" means no more in relation to the facts of the real world than a set of facts whereby the one person (who has the right) is able to oblige the other (who is under the duty) to let him do the thing claimed, or alternatively that the same first person (who has the right) obtains from the courts the power to force the reluctant other to let him do that thing that the right claims. According to Hägerström's formulation, if neither of these factual conditions arises, then the meaning of "right" remains empty and is meaningless. Thus a person who has a right to fish in a river running through another's land is exercising the legal right when he either (1) has the power to fish in the river and does so and the landowner forebears to interfere, or alternatively (2) the person with the right to fish goes to court to enforce his right against the reluctant landowner. Only in the two contexts of exercise or enforcement does the right become real. Everything else is theoretical only or, worse still, mythological: being the remnants of a primitive law given authority because of belief in its magical significance.

But at the same time Hägerström notices that such mythical elements do appear to have a strong influence over us. Some normal legal acts use these magical powers in order to make public changes in the status of people and things. Hägerström refers to these powers as "word magic". He gives the example in Roman law of *mancipatio*, whereby a Roman citizen who has, say, bought a slave from another citizen, would carry out a public transfer ritual whereby he would hold a set of scales (*libripens*) in his hand and strike one of the pans with a coin, uttering at the same time a particular formula of words. This ritual conducted in the Forum, would make public the otherwise purely private sale transaction. From the time of the performance of the ritual, everyone would recognise the slave as being the property of the new owner. While this illustration comes from Roman law, there may be analogies with modern Scots law where, for example, the purely personal rights and obligations created in a sale of land by the seller to the purchaser require to be registered before the rights become real and thus recognised and enforceable within society as a whole. The private agreement is not enough. And again, in almost all jurisdictions, the public ceremony of marriage converts a private agreement between the bride and groom into a publicly recognised change of status. That public rituals can have such powerful effects is due to the fact that they make use of strong psychological forces.

Lundstedt

Anders Vilhelm Lundstedt was perhaps the most extreme of the Scandinavian Realists in his rejection of metaphysical elements. Laws are abstractions when considered away from the context of their use. They are "simply the facts of social existence". Laws ensure social welfare by drawing a balance among certain fundamental economic interests: freedom of action, persons, property, material life, and so on. To talk of legal rights is merely an abstraction from such processes: merely "labels" for what the legal processes achieve. Neither does justice have any real meaning, for it is nothing more than the social welfare that the legal processes are aimed at balancing. Justice is little more than subjective reflections on the balance of economic interests.

Olivecrona

Karl Olivecrona regarded laws and their operation as the abstract expression of psychological forces. For example, when one person has a right, he feels that he has a power. A person under an obligation or duty feels subject to the power of others. Olivecrona criticised Austin's Command Theory as defective because while a command is, properly speaking, an order addressed by one person to another person, laws are not like this. Laws are addressed to society as a whole and all citizens (and officials) feel bound by them. The proper understanding of law is that the law merely expresses its content in the form of a command – in imperative form. But laws properly understood are the commands of no-one. Olivecrona says that they are "independent imperatives". A legal rule has two elements: the *ideatum* (the purpose which the legislator has in mind and to which the law is aimed) and the *imperatum* (the command-like form of expression of the rule). State officials use psychological forces in the form of laws to influence the actions of citizens. Provided that such laws are properly grounded in constitutional procedures, they have authority and will be regarded as "law" and followed by the citizens. Citizens will thereby feel bound by the law and will appropriate it in their actions. It is the performance of a certain formality of procedure involved in making law which gives laws the benefit of the psychological pressure needed to give the law its binding power. Olivecrona gives a number of examples of how the authority of a law depends on the proper constitutional procedures being followed. He gives the example of the naming of a ship. If, in the middle of the naming ceremony, a radical were to grab the champagne bottle out of the hands of the dignitary who was to name the ship, and smash the bottle against the side of the ship and say "I name this ship the *Generalissimo Stalin*" we would not feel that the ship was properly so named. Again, Olivecrona gives the example of a marriage ceremony: "centering upon a few performative words which purport to make the parties man and wife. What happens? The psychological effect is instantaneous, uniform and far-reaching. Everybody falls into line and regards the newly wedded couple as man and wife".

Citizens use laws which they feel bind them in order to organise their social behaviour. The psychological pressure arises from the knowledge that something is the law. The "effect of [this] attitude towards the constitution is first, that the constitutional law-givers gain access to a psychological mechanism, through which they can influence the life of the country; secondly, that only they gain access to this mechanism and that everybody else is debarred from using it or building up another system".

When examining the effect of a law, we may analyse this by having "an idea of an imaginary action by a judge in an imaginary situation". The effect of a law can only be understood by imagining the action that the judge will take if faced by an accused found to have broken a rule. But this may be a difficult task for Olivecrona recognises that no rule stands on its own, and no decision is capable of being made on the basis of the consideration of one rule in isolation. Sometimes psychological pressure is not enough to bind citizens and coercion is required so that officials can force people to accept that the law is binding and to ensure compliance. Olivecrona says: "in every community force is consistently applied through the officials of the state more particularly in three forms; police measures against disturbances, infliction of punishments and the execution of civil judgements. In all three cases physical violence or coercion is the ultimate expedient".

Olivecrona believes that there is a necessary relation between law and morality. Morality does not influence law; rather, it is the other way around. Indeed, law creates morality. Everyone

> "grows up in a community where legal machinery has existed since time immemorial ... The character is formed under the influence of our surroundings ... among the forces working within society the law is without doubt one of the foremost. The law certainly cannot be a projection of some innate moral convictions in the child, since it has existed long before he was born. The first indelible impressions in early youth concerning the relations to other people are directly or indirectly derived from the law. But the effect is not only to create fear of the sanctions but also to cause that individual to adjust himself so as to be able to live without fear. The rules also have a positive moral effect in that they cause a deposit of moral ideas in the mind".

Ross

Alf Ross is principally remembered because of his analysis of the concept of "binding". Ross uses the analogy of a chess game. A third-party observer can see that the players are operating a system of rules but the third party does not know what those rules are. The players, on the other hand, not only follow the rules but regard themselves as bound by those rules. They feel psychologically bound by them. The rules have a normative power. If one of the players breaks a rule of the game then that is the basis for criticism. Law provides social meanings and this is the justification for the feelings of binding when choices of action are made by citizens or when officials act to enforce a rule. Laws are thus addressed not merely to citizens (where they set standards of behaviour to be followed) but to the officials who must exercise the coercive powers in the event of disobedience by a citizen. The use of coercion is of particular importance since the work of officials and the courts is primarily a matter of the use of force. Citizens who obey the rules do so for a range of motives such as feelings of being bound by the law, feelings of duty to obey the law, or fear of the consequences of disobedience in terms of the sanctions that will be imposed by officials. Officials such as judges obey the rules because they feel bound by the constitution and the acknowledged sources of the law. These functions are two aspects of the same rule so that there is no need to employ a double set of norms one addressed to citizens and the other to officials. In this way Ross to some extent parallels Hart's treatment of the internal and external aspects of rules and at the same time parallels Kelsen's idea of laws being rules directed to officials. Throughout, however, Ross is clear that these feelings of rightness and wrongness of action are merely psychological feelings and they have no ultimate objective reality. As a result, Ross describes the idea of justice as being no more than strongly held subjective feelings of being bound. He says that justice is no more than "banging upon the table", as it were, in emphasis of one's approval or disapproval of the matter in hand.

Essential concepts

- Realists react against the idea of law as a set of axioms, rules and forms. They believe that law is truly revealed when law is in action.

American Realism

- Oliver Wendell Holmes looked at the way in which judges make decisions. Uncertainty about the outcome of a case is caused by the uncertainty about the way that judges will apply the rules. This is called "Rule Scepticism".
- True law only exists when the judge determines a case but some idea of justice will be in the judge's mind when he interprets the rule. A judge may be influenced by moral, political and social principles, and perhaps the particular prejudices which the judges share with the common man and woman.

- Case law which is built up over time is far more real than the textbooks, statutes and principles. This is because judge-made precedent is a record of legal rules interpreted by judicial principles and applied to actual factual situations.

- Holmes's "Bad Man" does not care about textbook legal argumentation. He only wants to know what the outcome of the case will be – what the judge will decide.

- Frank thought that uncertainty about outcomes depends on the facts which the judge or jury hold to be true. The application of rules is comparatively simple thereafter. This approach is known as "Fact Scepticism".

- In deciding what facts to hold, judges (and juries) may be prejudiced by racial, religious, economic or political factors, and other non-obvious factors too possibly including a judge's class, education, and religion.

- Both Rule Sceptics and Fact Sceptics are pessimistic about the possibility of predicting the outcome of court decisions, but for different reasons.

- Llewellyn saw the purpose of a legal system as providing society with the tools that it needs in a changing world, assuring the survival of the members and the maintenance of order and justice.

- Llewellyn identified a number of "law jobs": dealing with "trouble" cases and restoring order ("garage repair work"), channelling conduct and expectations so as to avoid trouble and to allow people to adjust to social change, providing members of society with integration, direction and incentive, providing authority and authoritative procedures, creating judicial methods aimed at the settlement of disputes.

- Llewellyn said that there were two styles of judging. First, a "formal" style sticking rigidly to rules and applying them logically which may result in injustice. Second, a "grand" style where judges apply a "situation sense" and look at the purposes of the rules and other policy considerations and attempt to do justice. In the "grand" style, the judge draws upon professional and cultural ideals generally held within the legal profession and society.

- Schubert analysed scientifically a judge's background, temperament, economic status and attitudes. He used his conclusions to explain the decisions in some prominent legal cases.

- Loevinger devised Jurimetrics which is a mathematical analysis of legal decision-making systems. He regarded a court as an open system interacting with its environment and consisting of inter-related parts. The personnel of a court (judge, counsel, defendant, jury) all have their part to play, as do the various interrelated rules and procedures. Decision-making therefore involves a large set of complex factors. Activity such as failure within part of the whole system will affect the other parts.

Scandinavian Realism

- The Scandinavian Realists were particularly interested in the concepts of rights and obligations and asserted that these essentially involve situations where people orient their behaviour as a result of these concepts and in particular where rights are exercised or enforced.

- Hägerström thought the language of law is nothing but illusion. He examined the concepts of rights, duties, obligation, property, justice and so on, using a methodology that he likened to an onion. Just as an onion is made up of layer upon layer, so he hoped to strip metaphysical elements away from legal concepts in order to find the inner factual content.

- Hägerström noticed that mythical elements do appear to have a strong psychological influence over us and enable us to ritualise public changes in the status of people and things. These may be called "word magic".

- Lundstedt thought that laws are simply the facts of social existence. They ensure social welfare by drawing a balance among certain fundamental economic interests.

- Justice has no real meaning. It is little more than subjective reflections on the balance of economic interests.

- Olivecrona regarded laws and their operation as the abstract expression of psychological forces.

- While a command is an order addressed by one person to another person, laws are addressed to society as a whole and all citizens (and officials) feel bound by them. They are merely expressed in imperative form. They are the commands of no-one. They are "independent imperatives".

- A legal rule has two elements: the *ideatum* (the purpose which the legislator has in mind and to which the law is aimed) and the *imperatum* (the command-like form of expression of the rule).

- State officials use psychological forces in the form of laws to influence the actions of citizens. Provided that such laws are properly grounded in constitutional procedures, they have authority and will be regarded as "law" and followed by the citizens. Citizens will thereby feel bound by the law and will appropriate it in their actions.

- Law-givers gain access to a psychological mechanism, through which they can influence the life of the country. Only law-makers can do this. Everyone else is debarred from using it.

- When examining the effect of a law, we may analyse this by having "an idea of an imaginary action by a judge in an imaginary situation" – imagining the action that the judge will take.

- No rule stands on its own, and no decision is capable of being made on the basis of the consideration of one rule in isolation.

- Sometimes psychological pressure is not enough to bind citizens and coercion is required so that officials can force people to accept that the law is binding and to ensure compliance. This may involve police measures against disturbances, infliction of punishments and the execution of civil judgements. In all three cases, physical violence or coercion is the ultimate expedient.

- Olivecrona believed that law influences morality. Among the forces working within society, the law is without doubt one of the foremost. We learn about the imposition of rules in early youth. But the effect is not only to create fear of the sanctions but also to cause that individual to adjust himself so as to be able to live without fear. The rules have a positive moral effect in that they cause a deposit of moral ideas in the mind.

- Alf Ross analysed the concept of "binding". Ross uses the analogy of a chess game. A third-party observer does not know what it is like to be bound by rules. Only those who are bound by rules feel the psychological binding power.

- If one of the players breaks a rule of the game then that is the basis for criticism. Law provides social meanings and this is the justification for the feelings of binding when choices of action are made by citizens or when officials act to enforce a rule.

- Laws are also addressed to officials who must exercise the coercive powers in the event of disobedience by a citizen.
- Feelings of rightness and wrongness of rule-ordered action are merely psychological feelings and they have no ultimate objective reality.
- The idea of justice is no more than strongly held subjective feelings of being bound. Justice is no more than "banging upon the table", as it were, in emphasis of one's approval or disapproval of the matter in hand.

6 LAW AND SOCIETY: HISTORICAL, MARXIST, ANTHROPOLOGICAL AND SOCIOLOGICAL THEORIES

This chapter looks at four different types of related theories:

(1) Historical theories see law as a product of a historical evolution and try to explain the law in terms of hidden forces which affect society.

(2) Marx explains history as a conflict between classes and sees law as a tool of oppression used by a privileged bourgeoisie who use it to oppress the proletariat.

(3) Anthropological theories explain the law as a necessary part of human social interaction which is revealed by participating in the lives of (say) small tribal units as they battle to survive in a hostile environment. It thereby sets out to analyse and explain the environmental forces and the social responses of the examined society. This is done in terms of the behaviour, beliefs and understandings of the society members and the functions of the institutions of the society. General truths about law can be derived from its importance in simple societies.

(4) Sociological theories seek to explain society and its institutions (and so the law as one of its institutions) in terms of the socially organised behaviour and functions of individuals, groups and institutions within society using social scientific methods.

All that can be achieved in short compass is to give an overview of the leading ideas and thinkers.

HISTORICAL JURISPRUDENCE

The historical theorists believed that a proper explanation of law requires to take into account the history of the people within which law arises and functions. The appropriate methods to use should be historical methods. History explains the evolution of a society in terms of the spirit or essence of a people and this is reflected in the institutions of the society of which law is one. We look at two thinkers: Friedrich Carl von Savigny (1799–1861) and Sir Henry Maine (1822–88).

Carl von Savigny

Savigny was a German historian who believed that history is explained by the evolution of the values and life of the members of a society and not by the exploits of a set of elite individuals such as monarchs and generals. This was a break from the previous historical methodology and makes him one of the founders of the European historical school. In Savigny's view societies evolve their own values which are rooted in the society's history and in particular in its traditions, culture and institutions. Law is a product of this and an important social institution. Savigny recognised that in German societies (the state of Germany did not come into existence until 1871 but had previously been a loose collection of German lands, principalities and territories) legal systems were rooted in Roman law which was adapted to the particular cultural conditions of the society. However, after Napoleon's various European conquests, areas under French control and authority, such as the Rhine Confederation and Prussia, had the French *Code Civil* imposed upon them with no consideration for the culture, values and needs of the subjugated peoples. Savigny was deeply hostile to this imposition.

Savigny characterised the history of the German peoples by reference to their Peoples' Spirit or *"Volksgeist"*, by which he meant the common customs and popular feelings of German peoples. In his view, law, as one of society's social institutions develops in parallel with the common consciousness of the people who form the society. The *Volksgeist* is an important influence on the development of the law. Law evolves with the evolution of society, it is strengthened when a society gains in strength, and equally as a society dies away and loses its identity, so the law also ceases to function. This is because a people require the law to deal with their problems and hopes and law-makers and judges who are members of the society bring their historically mediated understandings and experience into the process of law-making and law interpretation.

To establish his theory, Savigny looked at the evolution and disintegration of the Roman law. In his writings he asserts that Roman law was formed out of the customs and popular feeling of the Roman people – the Roman *Volksgeist*. This was a study of a particular historical civilisation (stretching over roughly a 400-year period) and an interpretation of the Roman law which today is generally thought to be somewhat selective and lacking in objectivity in some areas. From this particular study Savigny derived general conclusions. He considered that Roman history exemplified necessary stages in the rise and fall of all societies. Methodologically, this is deriving a general hypothesis from a particular instance which is the inverse of normal laws of implication.

Savigny considered that all societies go through three main stages and that this is manifested in the legal system. First, the beliefs and values that unite the people into the society develop customary legal solutions. Second, the law reaches its height and becomes codified and professionalised giving rules of general and detailed application. And third, legal systems start to decay. This general typology then enabled Savigny to interpret and describe the *Volksgeist* of the German peoples and to show how the law reflected their values and was fitted to their needs, customs and values.

Savigny's theory is open to several forms of criticism. His methods are suspect. His interpretation of history contradicts the fact that rulers do impose laws which may have little to do with the people. There are many examples in history, even in Roman history, where one people has subjugated another and imposed their culture, values and laws regardless of the culture of the latter. Savigny has little interest in legislation. He writes:

> "All law is originally formed in the manner in which, in ordinary but not quite correct language, customary law is said to have been formed: that is that it is first developed by custom and popular faith, next by jurisprudence – therefore, by internal silent operating powers, not by the arbitrary will of the law giver."

Clearly, a system of courts and precedent is better suggested by his theory. Savigny thinks that law-makers do not impose a will of their own but act as conduits for the values of the people. He also does not clearly define a *Volk* and we are left wondering if there really can be such a thing. What, for example, would a British *Volksgeist* look like? What are the beliefs, values and cultural elements of the British people? Is it realistic to suggest there is such an identifiable unity within the United Kingdom given that it consists of several countries with their own historical identities? Nevertheless, Savigny's contribution to jurisprudence is important. There are social pressures which reflect community consciousness and beliefs which will inform the legislation and governance of modern states. Law does reflect social attitudes. The interpretation of social culture and values was a stimulus to the development of anthropological and sociological studies to come.

Sir Henry Maine

Maine was a lawyer and historian and brought his knowledge of ancient Greek and Roman history and his experiences in India to bear upon his study of law. As a result, his methods are comparative and not restricted to one legal system. He was also influenced by Darwin's *Origin of Species* and so felt that ideas of evolution derived from biological contexts could be extended to explaining the evolution of societies and their systems of law. Unlike Savigny, Maine considered that there were six identifiable stages which legal systems could pass through in the evolution of the society in which they arose. However, stagnant societies would pass through only three stages while progressive ones would pass through all six.

In the first three stages the law develops spontaneously. The stages are as follows: First, patriarchs would impose their will on the people, claiming that their judgments were divinely inspired. Often the sovereignty of the patriarch also depended upon such beliefs. The original judgments would be decided as ad hoc solutions to particular problems and not show any developed patterns of thinking. They would appear more like commands and opinions than judgments. Second, the authority of the original divine inspiration would become diluted and decision-making would become delegated to aristocrats. Royal judgments would be followed and become customary, allowing patterns of decision-making to be developed. Third, laws would become written and codified. In Roman law this corresponds to the creation of the Twelve Tables while in English law it corresponds to the innovation of law reports.

Progressive societies would then pass through the following stages which are marked by social and legal changes where law requires to evolve new solutions, while initially retaining the semblance of continuity with the past: Fourth, legal fictions are tolerated and then become the rule. Legal fictions are "any assumption which conceals, or affects to conceal, the fact that a rule of law has undergone alteration, its letter remaining unchanged". Their purpose is to advance the interests of justice. Fifth, equity develops as a separate body of rules with a higher standing to which all law should conform. Equity's purpose is to ameliorate the consequences of the rigid application of rules. Sixth, legislation, being the authoritative enactments of a legislature, becomes the norm, thus providing quick and original solutions to new problems. Maine described the general movement of a legal system through these stages as a movement "from status to contract". He meant that the members of the primitive society would gradually cease to be subservient subjects and would develop equality and so would be enabled to form free agreements with other citizens as equals. This change in legal relations would be reflected in the general evolutionary trend.

While Maine's methodology was an improvement upon that of Savigny, his six stages are a sweeping generalisation and not really borne out in history. Anthropological studies have also shown that "primitive" societies do not always develop along even the first three stages. It is also interesting that Maine does not envisage the decay of a society. His theory shows a gradual evolution towards an ever better future. Yet surely history tells a different story?

MARX AND JURISPRUDENCE

Karl Marx (1818–83) developed a world view based on a political and economic interpretation of history. History is the record of class warfare which shows an unstoppable progression towards a revolutionary transformation of society. There are three interwoven doctrines: first, dialectical materialism; second, the laws of economic production; and third, historical materialism.

Dialectical materialism

"Dialectical" is a term deriving from the philosophy of history of Hegel and means that truth is to be found in debate or dialogue between opposing propositions. Nothing exists on its own – isolated. Instead, everything exists in dialogue with other things and can only be understood in dialogue with those other things. Law, like everything else, is not static but demonstrates continual change often by a process of evolution by tiny increments so that individual steps are barely perceptible. To see that things are evolving requires that one takes the long view of history. For Marx, history shows the development of the struggle between the bourgeoisie and the subjugated proletariat. Dialectic is materialist in the sense that the world is a material object comprising material things and beings. This is a rejection of metaphysics. The material world and its material phenomena are entirely knowable through sense experience and experiment. Our knowledge of the world gathered through experience is therefore authentic. As a result of the dialectic, everything in the world is interconnected. Marx writes:

> "The material world perceived by the senses to which we ourselves belong is the sole reality ... our consciousness and thought, however supra-sensible they may seem, are merely the products of a material and corporeal organ, the brain. Matter is not a product of the mind, but the mind itself is merely the superior product of matter."

When we ask how such a world can be interconnected, the answer is that, so far as law and human society are concerned, things are related because of the economic and political control by the bourgeoisie of labour and capital.

The laws of economic production

Under capitalism, production is regulated by economic laws. There are two sorts of people: bourgeoisie and proletariat. The bourgeoisie, the capitalist elite, own the instruments of production and exploit these to derive profit out of the labour of the proletariat. The proletariat have no possessions of their own. They have only their labour to sell. The process is exploitative. As time progresses, the bourgeoisie become wealthier and more powerful while the proletariat become poorer and less empowered. The gulf between the two classes widens continually. The legal system is created and controlled by the bourgeoisie and the purpose of laws is to perpetuate this system and keep the proletariat under domination. Laws are a means of oppression of the proletariat. Ultimately, the widening gap in terms of wealth and power and the process of exploitation reaches a stage where the proletariat finally recognise their predicament, gain the knowledge of their exploitation, and after becoming organised they rise up against the bourgeoisie and overthrow them and the society that oppresses them. Class divisions disappear. Even the idea of property and power will wither away. Every person becomes free and equal. This final state is known as Communism.

Historical materialism

This concept tells us that the above ideas are worked out in history. In the earliest days people are equal and all means of production are held in common. But with the increasing complexity and the growth of economic activity, this results in economic and political power becoming concentrated in the hands of a smaller and smaller number. Marx says that ideological perceptions and institutions will always lag behind such changes and so there must be repeated instances of re-alignment as society develops away from monarchic or feudal methods of control (where absolute power is held by single sovereigns), and develops into a bourgeois society where a merchant class controls labour and economic production and continues the process of wealth and power concentration. That the class warfare that this causes will end in revolution is inevitable and unavoidable. It is just as inevitable that classes will disappear and freedom and equality occur. Marx analysed history at great length to show these processes of transition. He thought that the transition from monarchy and feudalism to bourgeois society occurred in Britain in 1689, at the time when William and Mary ascended the throne in place of King James VII and II, for this was when power transferred from the monarch to Parliament.

Despite Marx's detailed analysis and exposition, things did not take the course that Marx envisaged. The Bolshevik revolution took place in Russia in 1917. But it was not followed by equality and the disappearance of power and property. Some suggested that the final Communism was an end state which would be reached only after a period of transition and reorientation. "Communism" remained a major political and ideological force in the world for 70 years, until centralised politics and organised production finally collapsed in and around 1990. At that time former Communist states reverted to the values of Capitalism. The Communist dream of equality could not withstand the fact that individuals are basically competitive and greedy and no system of equality was able to withstand the desire of citizens to build up their own wealth and independence.

Nevertheless Marx's grand ideology proved to be the most influential non-religious ideology on the planet (always assuming that Capitalism is not regarded as an ideology). Marx's interpretation of history is similar to those of the Historical school of jurisprudence because of its use of historical methods and because it attempts to formulate an authoritative global explanation of history in which the values of the present are explained in terms of evolution from the past by means of hidden forces. For Marx, there was in addition an inevitable future utopia. Societies in all of these historical views are launched along a course of uni-directional progression. In each case present stages are the product of previous stages and the present leads inexorably to the next. Such thinking can also be found in some liberal views of the world that suggest that things are always getting better and the future lights the path towards utopia. But such an optimistic view is by no means necessary. There is no need to think in terms of inevitable progress. Perhaps there are other reasons for life feeling better today than in the past. Perhaps our present comfort is due to a cheap and plentiful supply of fossil fuel?

Marx on law, property and state

Given that, prior to the revolution, the bourgeoisie are engaged in gathering all power and profit for themselves, it is no surprise to find that Marx considers power and property to be instruments of oppression.

Marx defines the law as an instrument of class domination which allows the bourgeois class to control the proletariat by the use of force. It follows that laws, precedents, and courts, while having the appearance of a disinterested, beneficial system enforcing equality among citizens, are really nothing but a system of class domination. Marx says in the Communist Manifesto (1848):

> "Your jurisprudence is but the will of your class made into a law for all, a will whose essential character and direction are determined by the economic conditions of existence of your class ... behind your jurisprudence is your concern for the maintenance of your economic superiority. Your law is a mere expression, a rationalisation, of that concept."

Likewise, the state is nothing but an instrument used by those who control production and justifies the continued use of coercive legal power to continue class dominance. Law and state are effectively the same thing – both expressions of class dominance.

Property is a fiction invented to justify the possession and control of economic resources by the bourgeoisie. For as long as the bourgeoisie own these, they can prevent the proletariat from acquiring them. This is rigorously enforced by legal coercion. This maintains the status quo where the bourgeoisie is in control. In *Human requirements and the division of labour* Marx writes:

> "under private property ... every person speculates on creating a new need in another, so as to drive him to fresh sacrifice, to place him in a new dependence and to seduce him into a new mode of enjoyment and therefore economic ruin. ... Man becomes ever poorer as man, his need for money becomes ever greater if he wants to master the hostile power. The power of his money declines in inverse proportion to the increase in the volume of production: that is, his neediness grows as the power of money increases".

It follows that once proletariat gains a true understanding of the role of property, law and state it is inevitable that the proletariat will seek to remove these together with their oppressors. That is why revolution is inevitable.

Ultimately, Marx's ideology suffers from being too vast a theory in scale and one that ignores fundamental human motives for action. But he, like the historical theorists, shows that law can have a context within history, is a system of evolving values, is very much connected with the distribution of power, and may be used to maintain political and economic control by a self-serving political elite. These ideas have revived in more recent times with the Critical Legal Studies movement and Postmodern thinkers, as we shall see.

ANTHROPOLOGICAL JURISPRUDENCE

A completely different way of looking at societies and laws was proposed by anthropologists. Rather than recording and analysing the evolution of societies through historical stages, anthropologists looked at how societies live in the present time. Their methods involved participating in the life of a culture and thereby they were in a position to catalogue its activities, beliefs and values. They realised that even in "simple" societies the main struggle was survival. This was achieved by sets of mutual understandings exemplified in rule-ordered behaviour. Rules functioned like laws. Failure to fulfil expected obligations would result in sanctions by others in the society. While many of the studied tribal cultures were very different from Western society, the same basic structures and institutions could be discerned. In recent times anthropological studies have fallen out of favour, but they were important in showing how societies function. Anthropologists believed that the only way to understand a society was to look at the functions of its institutions. The aim was to document a whole cultural system and explain it in terms of interconnected elements and functions. Everything in a culture had its function which supported the general aim of survival. If anything ceased to perform a role in survival it would become redundant and cease to exist. Law-like rules exist in every culture and perform the role of enabling mutual understandings among the members of the culture. The rules also force people to follow general patterns of behaviour where these are critical for survival. Conclusions drawn from these anthropological studies can be applied to complex Western societies too. The right way to understand law and legal institutions is to look at how these function within Western societies.

Bronislaw Malinowski (1884–1942) was a leader of this school of thought. He studied the cultures of peoples in the Trobriand Islands near Papua New Guinea, looking at the rules of behaviour within their societies. Participation is necessary for a proper understanding of the life of the observed society. It gives an insider view and so what it feels like to be guided and follow the rules. Rules were considered to have binding force. They were not simply habits or customs. Malinowski's detailed analyses are an example of early types of "scientific" case studies. His methods provided analytical tools which came to be adopted by the later sociological theorists. Malinowski was concerned to show how the behaviour and rules of a society depended on their culture, beliefs and values. He showed the importance of understanding the ways in which societies explain their own existence. Societies do not come into existence fully formed. They develop over lengthy periods of time during which members of the society explain their behaviour and rules using a range of myths and motifs. Religion plays an important role in the development of a culture. If the behaviour and rules of societies could be explained only by looking at shared beliefs, myths and motifs, then such shared meanings could not be ignored when studying the functions of law in more complex societies such as those in the West. Religion retains strong explanatory roles within any society and provides values which inform a society's customs and institutions.

SOCIOLOGICAL JURISPRUDENCE

Having seen how methods were developed for historical and anthropological case studies, we now turn to sociological methods. We shall look briefly at some early sociologists and then make a more detailed study of the sociological legal work of Weber whose work is of enduring importance.

Some early sociological theorists

Auguste Comte (1798–1857) is sometimes regarded as the originator of sociology. He developed methods of study which centred upon the roles and understandings of individuals within society. He wrote: "Sociology itself depends upon preliminary study, first of the outer world, in which the actions of humanity take place, second of man the individual agent." In other words, he examined the external environment of society (the forces acting externally upon society) and also the internal environment. With regard to the latter, Comte set out to explain what it was like to be a member of the society. He did this by examining the role and actions of individuals. The particular methods he used included observation, experiment and comparison which he combined with the historical method. He was greatly interested in science as well as law and philosophy. He wrote both scientific and sociological works. His sociology is greatly indebted to the historical theorists and he conceived of French society as having passed through three stages: (1) theological (where fictitious supernatural beliefs dominated); (2) metaphysical (abstract beliefs in universal rights dominate); and (3) positive (authority becomes vested in scientifically justifiable laws).

Rudolf von Jhering (1818–92) was a "social utilitarian" who sought to explain law in terms of its social purposes. Law sets out to make a utilitarian balance between the interests of society on the one hand and the rights of the individual on the other hand. An important element for law is in minimising the situations in which these two interests conflict. Conflict is, however, inevitable and when this occurs the interests of society must prevail. But at the same time the needs of individuals within society remain very important. Jhering defined law as "the sum of the conditions of social life in the widest sense of the term, as secured by the power of the state through the means of external compulsion". This definition makes it clear that Jhering saw legal rules essentially as a means of compulsion and force. The social values and social utility which law protects preserve the goods and pleasures which individuals desire and which give life its meaning and value. These goods and pleasures include honour, art, science and so on. Every legal rule has a social purpose in resolving a conflict between social interests and individual interests. Jhering's analysis of individual rights is of interest. He considers that a violation of an individuals rights involves a perceived attack on an individual's social worth and honour. The sociologist needs to study and understand interests in order to understand the purpose and function of the law. In connection with the struggle between individual and society, Jhering writes that "everyone exists for the world and the world for everybody". Law provides levers of social motion. First, there are "egoistical levers" which give both rewards (promises of personal gain which appeal to selfish interests of individuals) and punishments (threats of sanctions which encourage individuals to avoid undesirable conduct). Second, there are "altruistic levers" such as sentiment and duty (these correlate with ethical self-preservation). A co-ordinated use of these levers by the state makes the achievement of social ends possible through the balance of interests. Jhering considered the goal of law and state was to bring about a "partnership of the individual and society". As well as goods and pleasures, there are also needs. These involve extra-legal needs such as food, mixed-legal needs such as self-preservation, and purely legal needs such as the paying of taxes. Law also ensures an appropriate distribution of these needs within society. Where the law makes a proper balance of competing interests on a utilitarian basis there will exist social cohesion which is a matter of great importance.

Eugen Ehrlich (1862–1922) noticed that there was often a distinction between the formal sources of law and jurisprudence on the one hand and the "living law" on the other. The formal sources comprised the law as imposed by the courts. The living law comprised the acknowledged and practised customs and norms by which members of society actually organised their behaviour. The two types of law need not coincide. In view of this distinction, Ehrlich divided "norms for decision" (the laws contained in statutes, codes and common law decisions and which enable people in society to resolve disputes) and "norms for conduct" (which are the rules of behaviour which individual members of society relate to and follow). Ehrlich felt that the gap between the two was important and legislators ought to take account of the possibility of a gap between what they provide and what people do. Ehrlich set out to investigate this divide and to see whether there were areas of overlap or whether the two were irreconcilable. In the Czernowitz experiment, he organised a seminar on the living law as followed in Czernowitz in the Ukraine. Groups of Ehrlich's students were asked to investigate the practice of law in the area and they collected huge quantities of data about documents, local customs and practices, rules of succession to property within families and so on. At the conclusion of the experiment Ehrlich was able to show that there was indeed a profound gap between legal code on the one hand and the customs and behaviour of the people on the other hand. The dangers of such a gap is that when a legislature creates law which is separated from the customs and habits of society members, they run the risk that their laws will not be obeyed and the legislators will lose the confidence of the populace. Good law therefore has to minimise the gap between legal rules and customary values and habits.

Emile Durkheim (1858–1917) viewed law as an index of the level of development within a community. In simple and "primitive" societies, men and women recognised the need for mutual assistance and so a collective solidarity existed with individuals assisting each other. In such a society values would be uniform since all members of the society understood the nature of the need and the co-operation which they offered to assist one another. Accordingly, individualism would be relatively rare. However, with the division of labour in society, this close knit collective way of understanding collapsed and individualism came to the fore. Law becomes necessary to produce social cohesion. Law does this by setting out patterns of acceptable and unacceptable behaviour. These ideas derive first from the morality of the simpler social system but soon the law comes to symbolise that morality and to substitute for it a new system of ties, binding individuals into coherent groups within society. The law develops into the source of the social solidarity and becomes the standard of the moral – law sets the morality of the society. Durkheim says: "Everything which forces man to take account of other men is moral." It follows that an act is criminal when it is generally perceived as offending the collective conscience (defined as the "totality of beliefs and sentiments common to average citizens of the same society"). Members of society are not shocked because a conduct is declared criminal. But the conduct is criminal because society's collective conscience is shocked – because of the adverse effects of that illegal conduct on social cohesion within the society. Accordingly, punishment is seen as an act of reparation offered by the criminal to the feelings of the members of society. Law as the instrument of social cohesion performs other roles as well such as resolving conflicts in the distribution of goods.

Weber

Max Weber (1864–1920) is sometimes referred to as the "father of sociological method". This appellation is deserved because of the enduring importance of his methods and ideas. Weber was a lawyer and he gave a thorough analysis of law and its role in shaping modern society. Modern society is Capitalist. The origins of Capitalism are to be found in protestant Christianity. Protestant businessmen had been reluctant to enjoy the profits that were produced in their businesses. Protestantism frowned upon enjoyment which it regarded as frivolous while work was important and character building. This means that profits had to be ploughed back into the businesses thus increasing economic activity. At some stage the religious drive was replaced by economic drives but the work ethic remained. Business was a serious enterprise pursued on its own merits and was far more serious than merely a means of survival. This gave rise to capitalism. The work ethic was transformed into what Weber calls the "rationality" of modernity. Weber had a pessimistic view of modernity. Things seemed to be in a regression, getting from bad to worse, but there appeared to be no way out. This leads to disenchantment. We shall now look at some of these ideas and then proceed to examine the ideas of legitimate domination, the nation state and the law. We shall then briefly look at Weber's sociological method.

Modernity and the rise of rationalisation

Weber saw that life in a social epoch of immense complexity was producing vast advances in wealth and power, but modern men and women had lost the ability to live as fully rounded persons. Modern society was attacking tradition and custom and replacing them with reason, progress and, in the sphere of peoples' lives, economic knowledge and freedom. This is a mixture of good and bad forces and results. It would be through knowledge that modern man and woman would learn the true structure of things and become free from the domination of ideology and the other falsehoods of tradition and custom. But at the same time, and as a result of workplace ethics, the whole lives of individuals would become controlled by this same kind of reasoning. It would seem as if the magic and values of traditional life would have to surrender to rationality. The world would become more and more the subject of the empirical sciences, more and more known through generalities of description, often quantifiable description. This would cause areas of mythology and spirituality in life to disappear. The mythology of traditional life involved superstition and belief, values which have provided such fruitfulness and creativity in literature, poetry and the arts, and which could therefore be described as giving the "magic" or colours to life. These would ultimately disappear to be supplanted by workplace rationality. It is not that the mythical elements would be rejected by modern man, but merely that he would have no further use for them. So the creative colour which such myths and symbols gave to life would be lost for ever, replaced by the measurable, the statistical, and the mundane.

What is modernity? Due to the adoption of the workplace ethic, the world, a socially organised human structure, would become increasingly rationalised. Rule-ordered administration would become an ever increasing feature of modern Capitalist society. Capitalism would introduce ideas of economic rationality but its primary function was not to bring about rationality: its primary function was to control and create wealth. Industrial processes, the centres of wealth creation within Capitalism, were controlled by efficient workplace administration. Through this type of administration society too would develop. The workplace rationality arising within the workplace would become the rationality of bureaucratic administration and would come to challenge the ideology of law and revolutionise the rule of men. Weber wrote: "This whole process of rationalisation, in the factory as elsewhere, and especially in the bureaucratic state machine, parallels the centralisation of the material implements of organisation in the discretionary power of the overlord." Inevitably, politics would become imbued with this same rationality, and this would in turn affect the development of the modern state, and create a style of government in which reason, rather than any arbitrariness becomes the basis for decision-making.

Rationalisation would therefore occur in every sphere of human life and endeavour. It was inescapable, inevitable and positive. While it had strong links with Capitalism, rationalisation was not a necessary partner of capitalism. Rather, capitalism was a response in economic terms to this rise of rationality. The technologies which had built industrialisation were a product of it.

But Capitalism and the rise of Rationalism would inevitably bring about the spiritual poverty of human individuals. It would take away the natural rhythms and experiences of daily life; it would turn people into the tenders of machines, into cogs in the Capitalist machine, and so into the subjects and not the objects of administration and control. Weber thought that there were immense dangers in the inevitable loss of the mystery and meaning of traditional life. People were in danger of becoming nothing but rational machines: machines with brains but with no meanings or purposes other than work.

Rationalisation

What sort of thing was this rationalisation exactly and how would it succeed in rising within modern society? Weber thought rationality would come to dominate through three procedures:

(1) The control of the world would be brought about through economic calculation and the collecting and recording of information – the methods of accountant. In the business world this starts with book-keeping and the book-keeping mentality.

(2) The meanings and values would coalesce into an overall consistent explanatory scheme, a workplace knowledge which would be shown to be successful in the rise of Capitalism.

(3) The rationality of the workplace would supplant the natural ways of thinking in other areas of life creating a methodology of living in daily life according to rules. Rationality means living by rules of reason in the workplace. It becomes natural to fall into the same patterns of thinking in other areas of life. Living a rational life in everyday life would mean following rules of morality and law rather than acting on impulse or on emotion. It would mean building up a consistent rule-ordered rational picture of all areas of life and using this to give meaning and value to everyday life. Following this pattern through our lives to its conclusion, our actions would then be nothing but choosing the most efficient means to achieve our rational ends.

This way of thinking is very blinkered and leaves no room for superstition or religious belief and the other colours of traditional culture. Nor is there any remaining room for any non-scientific, non rule-ordered ways of thinking. While such rule-organised, empirically ordered and clearly definable means-to-ends thinking is easier than investigating other metaphysical ways of thinking, such easy rational methods would result in a general draining of traditional or customary richness in life. This is why Weber is pessimistic about life and society. There is no utopia to be striven after. We are reaching the only end that is possible – the rationality of modernity.

The nation state and legitimate domination

The emergence of modern rationality is also closely associated with the rise of the nation state. This is because Capitalism and nation state feed one upon the other. Weber says:

> "One can define the modern state sociologically only in terms of the specific means peculiar to it as to every political association, namely, the use of physical force. Every state is founded on force, said Trotsky. That is indeed right. If no social institution existed which knew the use of violence, then the concept of state would be eliminated, and a condition would emerge that could be described as anarchy in the specific sense of the word. Of course, force is certainly not the normal or the only means of the state – nobody says that – but force is a means specific to the state. Today the relation between the state and violence is an especially intimate one. In the past the most varied institutions have known the use of physical force as quite normal. Today, however, we have to say that a state is a human community that successfully claims the monopoly of the legitimate use of physical force within a given territory. Note that 'territory' is one of the characteristics of the state. Specifically, at the present time, the right to use physical force is ascribed to other institutions or to individuals only to the extent to which the state permits it. The state is considered the sole source of the 'right' to use violence. Hence 'politics' for us means striving to share power or striving to influence the distribution of power, either among states or among groups within a state."

The other institutions and individuals authorised to use the state's power of coercion involves principally public officials. Weber writes:

> "The bureau segregates official activity as something distinct from the sphere of private life … public monies and equipment are divorced from the private property of the official … the executive office is separated from the household, business from private correspondence, and business assets from private fortunes … [in the sphere of the bureau] the complete de-personalisation of administrative management by bureaucracy."

The state's systems of control based on its powers of coercion are sometimes referred to as "*Herrschaft*" which means "lordship" or perhaps "domination". Weber does not think that a state grounded purely on coercive domination would be stable. It requires to be regarded as legitimate by the subjects. The state's control should be seen as authoritative or commanding. Only then will the state be politically stable and effective in its actions. People feel that they should comply with such legitimate commands. This is achieved by three means:

(1) habit;

(2) belief by the people in the legitimacy of the commands – the law is the law; and

(3) people's considerations of expediency and possibly self-interest: law attains purposes which give economic opportunities which can be exploited by subjects.

In this way "legitimate domination" is achieved by both force and legitimate authority. So, sociologically speaking, Weber says that: "a *Herrschaft* is a structure of super-ordination and subordination, of leaders and led, of rulers and the ruled; it is based on a variety of motives and means of enforcement".

Typologies of legitimacy

But what types of legitimacy are there? Legitimacy arises in the response of the majority of the people to their leaders. It is a kind of belief in the leader's authority. Weber says that it has to have a foundation and different types of legitimacy have been exemplified in history. Weber identifies three types:

(1) **Traditional authority**: where established belief arises from the sanctity of immemorial traditions and the legitimacy of the status of those exercising authority under them. The origins are likely to be in traditional tribal, magical, or religious beliefs. This is the most ancient and has been the most widespread within world history.

(2) **Charismatic authority**: rests on devotion to specific and exceptional individuals due to their sanctity, heroism or exemplary character. The authority extends to the leader's patterns of decision and action. Weber thinks that this sort of authority is unstable and unpredictable because very often such leaders will act arbitrarily and their reigns may end in a power vacuum and a resultant period of political uncertainty. Individual leaders may

also generate rivalries and are not averse to overthrowing weak
opponents.

(3) **Rational–legal authority**: this is based on rational grounds
where there is a belief in the "legality" of patterns of normative
rules. Individuals rise by means of the rules to positions of
legitimate authority and so are thought to have the right to issue
commands. It is this type of legitimacy which dominates modern
western societies and which provides the most stable form of
government.

Modernity has at its heart rational–legal authority. It has a highly ordered
structure and involves certain characteristic features:

(1) A legal code consisting of legal rules accepted by the people
as authoritative by agreement or imposition or on grounds of
expediency. This is accepted by the majority or at least by the
most important and influential members of the society;

(2) A logically consistent system of abstract rules which allow norms
of general application to be applied in particular situations. This
allows the general norms to be applied to specific situations which
the general norms only addressed in general terms.

(3) The power of the state is administered by authorised officials
occupying administrative offices. These control mini-dominions
within which the official can exercise his powers but only so far
as those powers are authorized and constrained by the authorising
law.

(4) The subject is not a subject as a result of any person or individual
attribute, but only because he or she is a member of some social
group recognised and addressed by the law.

(5) People come to believe that it is the law that they are obeying and
not the officials who impose that law. Officials are obeyed only
because of the state's interests which they represent. The power of
state officials does not reside in them personally, but only in their
offices.

Seen as a state-wide organisation, rational–legal authority involves an
autonomous body of law in the form of a system of rules administered by
officials and which are habitually obeyed, because the laws are believed
in by the majority of the society who are ruled thereby. Legal decision-
making must be consistent and the law must be consistently administered.
Individual subjects are, as members of some social group or other, or

simply as members of that society, treated as equal since they are treated merely as subjects of law and not as individual persons.

Inequality and social justice

The law treats people as equals, but this does not mean that people are socially or economically equal. Class structures may persist and inequalities of power and property may also persist. The law need do nothing to alter this situation. It could easily perpetuate the status quo. It can perpetuate or even protect the interests of a bourgeois elite. Indeed it may give rise to feelings by the elite that they only receive what they deserve. The law therefore need take no interest in claims for social justice which may be made by the poor or lower classes. Indeed, it would not naturally do so. Weber writes:

> "The fates of human beings are not equal. Men differ in their states of wealth or social status or what not … but he who is more favoured feels the never ceasing need to look upon his position as in some way 'legitimate', upon his 'advantage' as 'deserved' and the others' disadvantage as being brought about by the latter's 'fault.' That the purely accidental causes of the difference may be ever so obvious makes no difference."

Social inequality within modernity is clearly caused by class differences, by differing access to wealth, political power and social status. These are a product of history. The legitimacy of the rational–legal state grew out of previous forms of legitimacy which, at least in its early years of rational–legal authority, will continue to influence it and provide support for its legitimacy.

Disenchantment

As we have seen, the essence of rationality is to supplant customary, traditional, religious, supernatural and metaphysical elements in the pursuit of a pure empirical understanding, a pure science of knowledge. But individual human motivations remain of this traditional sort. People therefore come to feel trapped by rationality. They are trapped by the processes and demands of the workplace and its ethic and ways of thinking. They trapped by their inherited class status, wealth and power – this is particularly felt by those who are of low social status, poor and un-empowered. People feel impoverished by the removal of the traditional magic and colour of life which gives meaning and value to their lives and actions. Weber said that modern man is "trapped in a cage surrounded by iron bars of rationality". This has effects within the law. Weber says:

"Legal positivism has, at least for the time being advanced irresistibly. The disappearance of the old natural law conceptions has destroyed all possibility of providing the law with a metaphysical dignity by virtue of its immanent qualities. In the great majority of its most important provisions, it has been unmasked all too visibly, indeed, as the product or technical means of a compromise between conflicting interests."

Law becomes little more than a tool used for control and discipline. Our mentality is affected and we learn to see ourselves merely as members of a mass whose duty is simply to obey. It should be no surprise that law provided opportunities for Communist and Fascist dictators.

Weber's sociology

Weber developed important sociological methods. People's actions are given meanings and purposes because of their subjective understandings in the context of their decision making. A sociologist therefore has to participate in society in order to understand and explain individual and social action. Weber says: "Science concern[s] itself with the interpretative understanding of social action and thereby with a causal explanation of its course and consequences." What must be examined is "the acting individual attaching a subjective meaning to his behaviour". An action is social "insofar as its subjective meaning takes account of the behaviour of others and is thereby orientated in its course".

We can see that social action involves relating and orientating ourselves with others. Sociologists need to understand the social relations involved in actions. The actor gives meanings to his or her actions. Sociologists need to understand these meanings. To achieve this Weber uses "*Verstehen*" which simply means "understanding". We must examine and understand the meanings of action. We must empathise with the actor and project what meanings a rational person would have for him or her to do the particular action concerned. We need to understand the subjective motivations for any action or relation. We can thus build up our understanding. This applies not only to individual actions and relations (which must be our starting point) but also regular types of individual and social actions, and ultimately we may then learn to understand pure or ideal types of common social phenomena and institutions or those of society as a whole.

Typologies of law

In examining law Weber distinguishes between Rational and Irrational forms of law. Rational ways of thinking involve scientific knowledge which liberates us from metaphysical entities and superstitious beliefs. Weber also distinguishes between Formal and Substantive systems of law. Formal systems are rule ordered and are built up out of codes and laws. Within a formal system, officials administer the rules and ensure compliance by means of the imposition of sanctions for disobedience. Substantive systems are based around principles of law and justice (such as equity). Formal systems have proved the most efficient.

Given that there are two types of rationality and two types of systems, there are four logical combinations (see Figure 6.1):

	Rational	Irrational
Substantive	Substantively Rational	Substantively Irrational
Formal	Formally Rational	Formally Irrational

Figure 6.1   Weber's typologies of law

(1) **Substantively irrational law**: In legal systems of this type, law is based upon decisions which are made ad hoc and addressed to the facts and circumstances of a specific problem which they answer. Decisions are made without reference to principles of law – indeed, there will be none. The method of decision making is irrational and non-scientific and will be based on ethical, emotional and political considerations.

(2) **Substantively rational law**: In this type of legal system, exemplified in theocratic legal systems, decisions are made within an authoritative system of justice but decisions will depend upon moral principles (of justice). As a result, law and morality will coincide. Because the system is rational, it is possible to systematise decisions and so a body of precedents can be built up.

(3) **Formally irrational law**: In this type of system, there are operative legal rules but decision making is not scientific and there will be recourse to irrational forms of decision. Such decision making may involve ordeal or oracle and other similar means which have no rational basis. Such methods of decision-making are likely to occur in simple tribal societies.

(4) **Formally rational law**: This is the highest type of legal system and is exemplified in the modern capitalist nations. There is a gapless system of law. Decisions are based on codes and decision-making is logical and scientific.

This typology is a useful way of analysing legal systems. It is wrong to think that it represents any sort of historical progression.

The historical development of legal systems

Weber is interested in historical development as a separate concern (as is seen in his study of forms of authority) and he provides us with a four-fold scheme showing the development of legal systems (not surprisingly, it is similar to the three-fold explanation of forms of authority but with an additional stage):

(1) **Charismatic**: Law is created by "law prophets" but the methods are magical or irrational.

(2) **Empirical**: Law is administered by people with special legal knowledge and skills. Decisions will still be somewhat *ad hoc* as no system of laws has yet come into existence.

(3) **Secular and theocratic**: Law is imposed by secular or theocratic powers. Justice is empirical in the sense that it is based upon previous decisions. However, the decisions are not yet rational. There is no system as the decisions have not yet been analysed nor principles abstracted.

(4) **Professionalised**: Law is administered by legal professionals who have a systematic view of the law and legal concepts. Decision-making is based on scientific and logical methods.

The legitimacy of the rational–formal legal system

Given what we have said above, it appears that modern rational–formal law needs to be understood in its historical context. The legitimacy of the system, like the legitimacy of the nation state is dependent on habit, force and considerations of expediency. Habit is often the strongest of these. To a great extent the habit of subjects of obeying the law gives the subjects the appearance of willing law's rule upon themselves. At first what is imposed, becomes held to be the natural way of things. The law is followed because it is the law. Members of a society give legitimacy to the laws by offering habitual obedience to those laws. More rarely obedience will be explained by reference to the values that law expresses. And even more rarely still, expediency will enter in. Weber writes:

> "the validity of a given order means more than the mere existence of a uniformity of social action determined by custom or self-interest. If furniture movers regularly advertise at the same time as many leases expire, this uniformity is determined by self-interest ... However, when a civil servant appears in his office daily at a fixed time, he does not act only on the basis of custom or self-interest which he could disregard if he wanted to; as a rule his action is also determined by the validity of an order (viz. The civil service rules), which he fulfils partly because disobedience would be disadvantageous to him but also because its violation would be abhorrent to his sense of duty ... The context of a social relationship may be called an order if the conduct is, approximately or on the average, orientated towards determinable 'maxims'. An order may be called 'valid' only when the orientation towards these maxims occurs, among other reasons, because it is in some appreciable way regarded by the actor as in some way obligatory or exemplary for him".

Essential concepts

Historical jurisprudence

- Savigny believed that peoples evolve their own values which are rooted in the society's history and in particular in its traditions, culture and institutions. Law is a product of this and an important social institution.

- In German societies, legal systems were rooted in Roman law which was adapted to the particular cultural conditions of the society.

- Savigny used the word "*Volksgeist*" or "people's spirit" to refer to the common customs and popular feelings of a society's people.

- The *Volksgeist* is an important influence on the development of the law. Along with the *Volksgeist*, law evolves, is strengthened, or dies away. All societies go through these three stages.

- Savigny looked at the evolution and disintegration of the Roman law. From this particular study he derived general conclusions.

- Sir Henry Maine identified six stages in the evolution of legal systems. All systems would pass through the first three but only some would pass through the later three.

- In the first three stages (patriarchal, aristocratic and codified) the law develops spontaneously. Progressive societies pass through the later three stages (administration by legal fictions, equity and legislation). In these later stages law evolves new modes of problem solving.

Marx

- Marx developed a world view based on a political and economic interpretation of history. History is the record of class warfare between a Capitalist elite and an oppressed proletariat. There is an unstoppable progression towards a revolutionary transformation of society after which power, property and state would wither away.

- "Dialectical materialism" means that truth is to be found by considering things and people in debate or dialogue (dialectic) with other things and people. Nothing exists on its own. In addition, things that exist do so as material entities (rather than as spiritual or metaphysical entities – for indeed there are no real things that are spiritual or metaphysical).

- By "laws of economic production", Marx means that production and people are controlled by economic laws. There are therefore two sorts of people, bourgeoisie and proletariat. It is economics that distinguishes them and their actions. The proletariat have no possessions. They have only their labour to sell. The process is exploitative. All history is explained in terms of economics.

- By "historical materialism", Marx means that a study and proper interpretation of history demonstrates that societies develop because of economic forces. Marx goes to history to prove the truth of his theories. Ideological perceptions and institutions always lag behind such changes and there must be repeated instances of realignment as society develops away from monarchic or feudal methods of control into a bourgeois society where a merchant class controls labour and economic production and continues the process of wealth and power concentration.

- Communism finally collapsed in and around 1990. The Communist dream of equality could not withstand the fact that individuals are basically competitive and greedy and no system of equality was able withstand the desire of citizens to build up their own wealth and independence.

- Marx considered that law, power and property were instruments of oppression. Law's appearance of a disinterested, beneficial system enforcing equality among citizens, is really nothing but a system of class domination.

- Law and state are effectively the same thing – both expressions of class dominance.

Anthropological jurisprudence

- Anthropologists looked at how societies live in the present time. Their methods involved participating in the life of a culture and thereby they were in a position to catalogue its activities, beliefs and values. Participation is necessary for a proper understanding of the life of the observed society. It gives an insider view and so what it feels like to be guided and follow the rules.

- In all societies the main struggle was for survival. This was achieved by sets of mutual understandings exemplified in rule-ordered behaviour.

- While many of the studied tribal cultures were very different from Western society, the same basic structures and institutions could be discerned. The only way to understand a society was to look at the functions of its institutions.

- Law performs the role of enabling mutual understandings among the members of the culture. The rules also force people to follow general patterns of behaviour where these are critical for survival.

- Malinowski showed how the behaviour and rules of a society depended on their culture, beliefs and values. He stressed the importance of understanding the ways in which societies explain their own existence in terms of a range of myths and motifs.

- Religion retains strong explanatory roles within any society and provides values which inform a society's customs and institutions.

Sociological jurisprudence

- Comte set out to explain scientifically both the external and internal environment of society. He asked what it was like to be a member of the society. He answered this by examining the role and actions of individuals.

- He thought society passed through three stages: (1) theological (where fictitious supernatural beliefs dominated); (2) metaphysical (abstract beliefs in universal rights dominate); and (3) positive (authority becomes vested in scientifically justifiable laws).

- Jhering was a "social utilitarian" who sought to explain law in terms of its social purposes. Law sets out to make a utilitarian balance between the interests of society on the one hand and the rights of the individual on the other hand.

- Jhering defined law as "the sum of the conditions of social life in the widest sense of the term, as secured by the power of the state through the means of external compulsion".

- Law provides levers of social motion. There are "egoistical levers" which give both rewards and punishments and "altruistic levers". Legislators use these levers to achieve social ends possible through the balance of interests.

- The goal of law and state is to bring about a "partnership of the individual and society".

- Ehrlich thought there could be a gap between the formal sources of law (codes and precedents enforced in courts) on the one hand and the "living law" (customs and traditions) on the other.

- Legislators ought to take account of the possibility of a gap between what they provide and what people do. Such a gap is dangerous as laws might not be obeyed and legislators would lose the confidence of the people. Good law therefore has to minimise the gap between legal rules and customary values and habits.

- In the Czernowitz experiment, Ehrlich collected huge quantities of data about documents, local customs and practices, rules of succession to property within families and so on. Ehrlich was able to show that there was indeed a profound gap between legal codes and the customs and behaviour of the people.

- Durkheim thought that in simple and "primitive" societies, men and women recognised the need for mutual assistance and so a collective solidarity existed. In such a society values would be uniform since all members of the society understood the nature of the need and the co-operation which they offered to one another. Accordingly, individualism would be relatively rare.

- In advanced societies, individualism becomes prominent and law is necessary to produce social cohesion. Law does this by setting out patterns of acceptable and unacceptable behaviour.

- Law's values eventually replace traditional morality. Law's values are aimed at producing social cohesion.
- A criminal act offends the collective conscience. Conduct is criminal because it shocks society's collective conscience. Punishment is an act of reparation offered by the criminal to the feelings of the members of society.

Weber

- Weber thought that modern society was attacking tradition and custom and replacing them with a form of rule-ordered scientific reason. This "rationality" would provide true knowledge and free people from the domination of ideology, and the other falsehoods of tradition and custom. But it would also replace and remove the traditional values which gave magic and colour to life. This causes disenchantment. People feel enslaved by their situation.
- However, people would become controlled by this kind of reasoning.
- In modernity, all things would become organised and increasingly rationalised. Rule-ordered administration would become an ever-increasing feature of modern Capitalist society. Rules are required to control and create wealth.
- Rationality would expand into all areas of life, including politics. This expansion is inescapable.
- Under Capitalism, the nation state would rise. Nation states are founded on physical force. This may be delegated to public officials. Control based on coercion is known as "lordship" or "domination". The state's use of coercion is seen as authoritative or commanding. People feel that they should comply with such legitimate commands ("legitimate domination"). This is achieved by means of habit, belief and expediency.
- There are three types of legitimacy: traditional, charismatic and rational–legal. Rational–legal authority involves legal rules, abstract rules, officials, and belief in the authority of law. Legal decision-making must be consistent and the law must be consistently administered. Individual subjects are treated as equal since they are all equally subjects of the law.
- Social inequality within modernity is clearly caused by class differences, by differing access to wealth, political power and social status. These are a product of history. Class structures and inequalities of

power and property may persist. The law need do nothing to alter this situation.

- Weber developed important sociological methods. He uses "*Verstehen*" which simply means "understanding". We must examine and understand the meanings of individual and social action. We must first understand individual actions and relations, then general actions and relations, and finally pure or ideal types of common social phenomena and institutions.

- Weber distinguishes between Rational and Irrational forms of law. Rational ways of thinking involve scientific knowledge which liberates us from metaphysical entities and superstitious beliefs. He also distinguishes between Formal and Substantive systems of law. Formal systems are rule ordered and are built up out of codes and laws. This gives rise to four important logical combinations.

- Legal systems develop historically through four stages: charismatic; empirical; secular and theocratic; and professionalised.

7 CRITICAL LEGAL STUDIES, POSTMODERNISM AND FEMINISM

CRITICAL LEGAL STUDIES AND POSTMODERNISM

The reaction against formalism (that a rigid application of legal rules is the proper and only way to resolve conflicts and disputes) which we saw motivated the American Realists was to recur with the development of the "Critical Legal Studies" movement in the United States of America in the 1970s. Once again, there was a movement looking to see what was factually or socially real about law and the structures of the legal system. However, its principal activity was an attack upon liberal interpretations of the law that we shall see exemplified in Rawls's view of justice (below).

Why did it attack liberal views? Because it felt that such views, which on the surface appear beneficent, actually hide the true nature of legal systems which is to perpetuate the political and economic status quo and so retain power and wealth in the hands of a traditionally powerful and wealthy class. In many ways the Critical Legal Studies movement was fuelled by a Marxist fervour, and the leaders of the movement were politically radical, but the movement tended to be reactionary only: while it was destructive of liberal values, it did not put forward any firm alternatives.

The product of critical law theory is simply to enable us to see the true nature of liberal legalism. The movement's methodology is one of deconstruction: an attack on formalist modes of reasoning and understanding. To suggest that there is an alternative would mean adopting a particular ideology and to engage in the process of reconstruction which was not the aim of the movement. While the leaders of the movement could agree on deconstruction, they were ideologically diverse.

The movement considered that many features of the received law required to be exposed as mechanisms for oppression. To a great extent, the law deals with the concept of rights. But this language hides undesirable ideological commitments. When an individual claims their rights, there is an assumption that the claimant needs the right which is being denied them. Justice is called in to satisfy that need. The injustice which gives rise to the need being asserted by an individual, is, however, on a proper construction, as seen through the lens of the Critical

Studies movement, a product of ideology. It suggests that the law should concentrate on individual interests rather than collective ones. It suggests that the resolution of the problem is to be found in the law confirming the ascendancy of one individual over others who are subjugated to that individual's claim. It perpetuates a belief that society should be naturally structured in terms of individual interests in property and power while in fact these are pure political constructs. Worse still, in providing a judgment, a judge is promoting the interests of the political class from which he or she comes. The judgment may be couched in terms of rules, carefully interpreted statutory provisions and precedent, from which legal logic derives an answer by deduction. But the judge's choice between alternatives is only logical in its expression. The expression is justificatory. It is a means whereby the language of the law asserts that the decision is reasonable. Behind this solid reason and logic, the actual decision is made in order to maintain the established order and to protect economic and political interests embedded in the dominant culture within society. The law is therefore a tool for the oppression of subordinates by a dominant class. It is not merely judicial decision-making behaviour which is attacked but also the values and other assumptions hidden in the law. The concepts of property, of contract and of crime are equally open to such critical deconstruction. For example, Kairys writes: "contract law constitutes an elaborate attempt to conceal what is going on in the world ... like other images constituted by capitalism, [it] is a denial of painful feelings and an apology for the system which produces them". In contract law, we believe that individuals have freedom of contract, that they can choose whether or not to enter into agreements with others on an equal footing, and thereby acquire rights or allow themselves to be bound by obligations. In reality, contract law sets up a system intended to maintain a stable, political and economic regime. Contract law properly understood serves the purposes of capitalism and maintains the political dominance of governors. At this point law and politics coincide. It is little surprise that law tends to be conservative, that it maintains the political and economic status quo.

The law is not alone in upholding the hidden values of a dominant class. Language itself perpetuates such values. As we learn to live within society, we encounter these same values which become implanted within us. The values become real for us and infect our ways of thinking. This is referred to as "reification". What once was a value imposed politically becomes a received truth, gains general acceptance, is believed to be legitimate, and is finally thought to be natural, part of the way things have to be. Education is equally open to criticism. Curriculum choices are made by the holders of political power. Their values and morality are instilled into us and corrupt our ways of thinking.

The movement reserves particular venom for American liberal legal thought as a form of ideology. In reality, liberal legal thought is a collection of conflicting political judgments and power structures hidden under an apparently objective and principled exterior. For example, civil and political rights which are purportedly preserved in and guaranteed by the American Constitution – the rights of free speech, assembly, religion and democracy – are not in fact based on the idea of the freedom of the individual, but in reality are simply symbols which serve the political and economic requirements of those who hold power. Any rights or freedoms actually acquired by individual citizens are so acquired only incidentally, as though only a by-product of the hidden process of class dominance.

Sometimes the law will expressly be used to attain some political end. This was the case with McCarthyism. During the 1940s and 1950s, politicians in the United States of America became particularly concerned with the threat of Communism. The naturally conservative Government feared that the country was being infiltrated by Communist agitators who would try to bring down the Constitution and Government and who were disseminating Communist ideas. Under the political leadership of Senator McCarthy, the Government reacted (or over-reacted) by carrying out a systematic investigation into the actions and affairs of people who were suspected of Communist sympathies and who held positions of influence. Government employees, public figures, educators and trade union officials were the prime targets of investigation. Media attention centred upon Senator McCarthy, who stunned the establishment by producing a list of names of 205 persons employed in the State Department and who he claimed were Communist party members. Though these claims were to a great extent unjustified, many people were tarnished by suspicion and lost their employment, status and reputation. Some people were tried, convicted and imprisoned. The FBI was very much involved in pursuing suspects and J Edgar Hoover, its Director, was insistent that informers' names should be withheld. In some cases suspects were not told what the allegations against them comprised nor were they given the opportunity for cross-examining witnesses. Proceedings in the House Committee on Un-American Activities were conducted in public and witnesses were frequently subjected to unacceptable levels of intimidatory examination. It was claimed there were Communists active in the Hollywood film industry and a "Hollywood Blacklist" was thought to exist. The reputations of eminent film stars were tarnished. One of those was Charlie Chaplin, who was forced to leave the USA. The investigations amounted to a crusade against Communism and the attitude towards suspects was little short of a witch hunt. All this occurred long before the Critical Legal Studies movement was started, but it provides evidence of the law being used to pursue the political interests of a wealthy and powerful elite. Who is to say that this kind of abuse is not a common but usually hidden aspect of the law?

The Critical Legal Studies movement sets itself the task of criticising elements of the legal system, of exposing oppression and inequality and of explaining in terms of ideological factors how legal concepts and institutions come to have unacceptable effects. To achieve these ends, the movement draws upon a range of methods from politics, economics, linguistics, psychology (and psychoanalysis). This multi-disciplinary character produces a tendency to diffusion of ideas leading to ever-decreasing agreement of concepts.

The achievements of the movement can be seen in three main areas: First, unlawful or openly exploitative power structures existing within law and society should be exposed and undermined. This is a common Marxist ideal. Second, legal structures are re-interpreted to show that they contain ideological underpinnings perpetuating exploitation and unfairness and at the same time are aimed at maintaining the dominant culture. Frequently the movement's findings are acknowledged by legislators who proceed to amend the law to improve justice and fairness. Third, de-reification may be achieved: legal solutions which originally solved specific legal problems, may become stock solutions and structures generally applied thereafter. But the application of inappropriate principles frequently produces unfairness. By de-reification, such unfairness can be exposed and expunged. Thus the effects of the Critical Legal Studies movement are frequently beneficial and can improve the law.

Postmodernism is a more recent phenomenon, originating in art and literature, which shows a resurgence of interest in deconstruction. It is aimed at attacking sweeping general concepts and values. Individuals make sense of the world in terms of a continuous dialogue of narratives. The work of the French philosopher Jacques Derrida is particularly important in Postmodernism. Derrida inverts the usual forms and senses of language and so hopes to reveal truths and distortions which have previously been hidden. Postmodernist thinkers such as Michel Foucault and Jurgen Habermas have considered legal aspects of society. They react against the power politics of the modern bureaucratic state (which they claim wishes to control and oppress individuals), the universalisation of values, and the globalisation of markets. We shall see something of Foucault's ideas in our discussion of Punishment (below).

The Critical Legal Studies and the Postmodernists have together developed methods of criticism which have strongly influenced racial and feminist developments. We now turn to Feminist theories in their own right and as an illustration of the methods which have been developed.

FEMINIST THEORIES

Feminist jurisprudence seeks to reinterpret existing legal structures which are seen as male dominated ("patriarchal"). Society is dominated by men who have set out to disempower and oppress women whilst at the same time raising men to all meaningful positions of power and control. If this is so, then it is undoubtedly important that this problem should be addressed since women constitute one half of humanity and it offends against the principles of justice that a person, let alone a whole section of society, should be disempowered and oppressed.

All forms of Feminism reject "patriarchy" which is identified in many aspects of society. Janet Rifkin, in "Toward a Theory of Law and Patriarchy", defined patriarchy as "any kind of group organisation in which males hold dominant power and determine what part females shall and shall not play, and in which capabilities assigned to women are relegated generally to the mystical and aesthetic and are generally excluded from the practical and political realms". Any aspects of law which appear to promote male authority and domination must be exposed and criticised. There are also "gendered thought-patterns" to be found in language and legal discourse which need to be removed. Feminists have pointed to aspects of property law, delictual damages, and criminal law attitudes to domestic abuse as showing elements of male domination. Women who were married were unable to hold property in their own right until the Married Women's Property Act 1882. It was only about 130 years ago that women were first allowed to study at university and to graduate. Patriarchy has enabled the exploitation or subordination of women. Injustices must be exposed and opposed. Within the language of the law women have often been referred to as the "weaker vessel". This frequently occurred in legal cases and documents in the 19th century. One American constitutional writer wrote: "if marriage is to be permanent, the government of the family must be put by law and by morals in the hands of the husband". In the American case of *Bradwell* v *Illinois* in 1872 the judge wrote: "civil law as well as nature herself, has always recognised a wide difference in the respective spheres and destinies of men and women ... man is, or should be, woman's protector and defender. The natural and proper timidity and delicacy which belongs to the female sex makes them evidently under fitted for many of the occupations of civil life". These are examples of prevalent myths about women as the weaker sex. Many Feminists object to the generic term "man" and the pronoun "he" referring to individual persons. It is suggested that this raises male roles as the dominant and normal while diminishing female ones. If men and women are to be regarded as equal, such practices must be ended. Lorenne Clark pessimistically wrote that men are "naturally stronger and freed from the grinding necessities of biological reality". Women have historically been expected to give birth to, rear, care for and nourish children, do the household chores and support a husband. The law should no longer be used to perpetuate this situation: instead, it should be used to redress this imbalance. The Feminist jurisprudence movement set out to expose injustices, amend the law, liberate women, and reveal oppressive fictions and myths promoting a male superiority.

Patricia Cain breaks down Feminist jurisprudence into four types:

(1) **Liberal Feminism**, which seeks to use the law to liberate women from the domestic sphere and to provide them with opportunities in society and in particular in the employment sphere.

(2) **Radical Feminism**, which sees women as an abused class engaged in a class struggle against men. The abuses must be countered using law and affirmative action. An area which has gained much publicity has been the attack on pornography which is seen as demeaning and denegrating women and turning them into mere sex objects for male gratification.

(3) **Cultural Feminism**, which, unlike the two earlier types, acknowledges the unique nature of women and "talks up" their special gifts and the contribution they can make to social life. Theorists within this form of feminism emphasise the "different voices" of women and the uniqueness of women's social connectedness.

(4) **Postmodern Feminism**, which rejects the very idea of a "woman's point of view". To assert a woman's point of view is itself considered to be dangerous, as it tries to make women conform to a particular ideological viewpoint.

The successes of Feminists have been considerable and equality has been regained in a large number of areas of social life. But it is interesting to note that many changes took place long before the occurrence of any identifiable Feminist movement (for example, the right of women to the vote, the right of married women to hold control over their own property and the right to education). Some have suggested that the existence of a feminist movement may be an important stage in a gradual global movement of increased awareness of symptoms of social injustice and discrimination. We can only speculate as to where such a movement will take us and into what concerns it will lead.

Essential concepts

Critical Legal Studies and Postmodernism

- Critical Legal Theorists attack liberal notions of the law which they say hide the true nature of legal systems which is to perpetuate the political and economic status quo and so retain power and wealth in the hands of a traditionally powerful and wealthy elite.

- Using the methods of deconstruction we are able to see the true nature of Liberal Legalism. While there is deconstruction, Critical Legal Theorists do not agree on what should replace the deconstructed law, as this would suggest adopting a particular ideology.

- Mechanisms of oppression should be exposed. Rights language hides undesirable ideological commitments. Property is a product of ideology. It promotes individual interests. Collective interests are more important. Concepts of contract and of crime are also opportunities for oppression.

- Judges promote the interests of their own political class. A judgment may appear to be the product of rules and precedent but this is only logical expression and its function is justificatory. Actual decisions maintain the established economic and political order.

- The law is a tool for the oppression of subordinates by a dominant class.

- Language also perpetuates dominant values. As we grow and learn, these values become implanted within us. This is referred to as "reification". We come to think of these values as natural and as the way things have to be.

- Education is equally open to criticism. Curriculum choices are made by the holders of political power. Their values and morality are instilled into us and corrupt our ways of thinking.

- Rights of free speech, assembly, religion and democracy are not in fact based on the idea of the freedom of the individual, but are symbols which serve the political and economic requirements of the elite.

- The Critical Legal Studies movement is multi-disciplinary and draws upon a range of methods from politics, economics, linguistics, psychology and psychoanalysis.

- The Critical Legal Studies movement has been successful in various areas of law reform by exposing and undermining unlawful or exploitative power structures which exist within law and society. Exploitative and unfair ideological content has been exposed. Unsuitable procedures and stock solutions which cause unfairness have been removed.

- Postmodernism is a more recent phenomenon, originating in art and literature which shows a resurgence of interest in deconstruction. It attacks sweeping general concepts and values.

- Jacques Derrida inverts language to reveal truths and distortions which have previously been hidden.

- Michel Foucault and Jurgen Habermas react against the power politics of the modern bureaucratic state which control and oppress individuals. They also oppose the universalisation of values and the globalisation of markets.

Feminism

- Feminist jurisprudence seeks to reinterpret existing legal structures which are seen as male dominated while women are disempowered and oppressed.

- Patriarchy is any kind of group organisation in which males hold dominant power and determine what part females shall and shall not play, and generally exclude women from practical and political realms.

- Injustices have been found in property law, delictual damages, and attitudes to domestic abuse.

- Within the language of the law women have often been referred to as the "weaker vessel" or the "weaker sex".

- Women have historically been expected to give birth to, rear, care for and nourish children, do the household chores and support a husband. The law should be used to redress such imbalances.

- Liberal Feminists seek to liberate women from the domestic sphere and to provide them with opportunities in society.

- Radical Feminists see women as an abused class engaged in a class struggle against men. Law and affirmative action must be used to counter this situation.
- Cultural Feminists emphasise the unique nature of women and their special gifts, uniqueness and connectedness.
- Postmodern Feminists reject the idea of a "woman's point of view", as this suggests a particular ideological viewpoint.

8 RIGHTS

The language of rights is so common that we instinctively respond to it and use it, but what we mean by "rights" is not obvious and varies from context to context – often without our being aware of this. For example, we talk of anti-discrimination rights, the rights of women to have equal opportunity with men to take jobs, and the right of ethnic minorities to non-discriminatory treatment, and so on.

From the perspective of Scots law, the origins of rights are to be found in the Roman law. As soon as persons become recognised in Roman law, their ability to form legal relationships with others and their ability to own and deal with property become matters of legal recognition. The Roman law recognised that citizens could enter into voluntary contracts with other citizens. Thus arose the consensual contracts of sale, hire, partnership and mandate. Strictly, the Roman law did not recognise abstract rights as such, but it did allow citizens to raise court actions (*condictiones*) to enforce obligations owed by others. By extension, obligations could arise involuntarily as a result of a harm being done by one citizen against another. Such obligations, including what we would now regard as crimes as well as delicts, allowed an aggrieved citizen to raise an action of delict against the person who had harmed him. In connection with property, a citizen could raise an action *in personam* against another for payment of a debt and thus to obtain transfer to him of the property, while the rightful owner of property could raise an action *ad rem* against a person into whose hands the first party's property had unlawfully fallen.

Thus we find in Scotland the important distinction between personal rights and real rights. We also recognise that some rights arise as a result of obligations undertaken voluntarily while others arise as a result of obligations created by law. We recognise positive rights entitling a person to do a particular things and negative rights entitling a person to prevent others from doing a thing. Private rights are held by individuals while public rights are vested in the community at large. Perfect rights are those enforceable by law, while imperfect rights cannot – usually because such rights have lapsed. Primary rights are rights that arise directly (such as the right of property) while secondary rights (or accessory rights) are those that arise only so that a primary right can be enforced (as for example a right of access to land. The ownership of the land is primary while the right of access is accessory). Sometimes the rights we speak of belong to all individuals in our community (such as the rights to freedom of the person, freedoms of speech and assembly and the right to privacy, to a fair trial and so on), sometimes they refer to minorities within the community (such as rights of such minorities to non-discriminatory treatment), and sometimes to individuals (my right to demand or even sue for payment of a debt, or for damages when I have been injured). We need a way to understand these different kinds of rights.

In this chapter we shall first look at the foundation of rights arising in positive law, thereafter at the foundation of natural rights or human rights, and finally at an important theory of analysis of rights (that of Hohfeld) and its criticism by MacCormick.

LOCKE AND POSITIVE RIGHTS

Under the Roman law, abstract rights did not exist. Rights were only the ability that citizens had to raise actions for the enforcement of obligations or duties owed by others. The primary aspect was always the duty or obligation and never the right. This idea of duty persisted right up to the 17th century. This is why Natural Law rarely speaks of rights and why human rights and natural rights have not been recognised until comparatively recently. Rights really came into existence with Contractarianism. We saw Hobbes's formulation of the Social Contract in Chapter 2. Hobbes believed that all powers of citizens were transferred to the sovereign. He was a creature of his time. For him, peace and political stability were primary, while the rights and liberties of citizens were secondary. It was only when non-monarchical systems of power became a likelihood that people began to think seriously about the duties that people owed to a state, the powers that the state held, and the duties that the state owed in return to the citizens – and so to the rights that citizens could claim against the state. Such thinking was a novelty.

John Locke (1632–1704) had experienced the same political turbulence as Hobbes. In his two Treatises on Government, Locke was writing at a time when the Divine Right of Kings to rule was being questioned. Locke disagreed with the absolute power of the monarchy. He questioned how a monarch could have any rights at all over a citizen. Locke asked how the rights of the citizens could arise in the first place and what limitations should exist on the power held by the sovereign thereafter.

He starts with the same general mythological idea as Hobbes. In his Two Treatises on Government, Locke describes the state of nature. For Locke, the natural state of mankind was not "nasty" and "brutish". It was a state of perfect freedom for individuals. They had complete freedom of action and the ability to acquire or dispose of their property as they thought fit. It was a state of equality. There was peace rather than war. While a person had a complete right to act as they chose, they were not permitted to harm any other person. Locke writes that: "all the power and jurisdiction is reciprocal, no one having more than another ... without subordination or subjection ... reason ... teaches all mankind who will but consult it, that being all equal and independent, no one ought to harm another in his life, health, liberty or possessions". And yet, some do. In a natural state disputes can arise and citizens may take the law into their own hands. Individuals may defend themselves and their property but individuals are weak and often unable to defend themselves. After the Social Contract the sovereign holds the power of the community. The sovereign is therefore required to intervene. The citizen has rights against the sovereign state to require it to act in his defence. A sovereign will put in place magistrates to protect individuals and their property, to punish those who harm individuals, and to order reparation be paid to the person harmed. In this way we have the idea of a state Government set up in order to achieve a definite purpose: that of protecting the peace and preserving the life, health, liberty and possessions of the citizens who are all regarded as equal under the law.

But how much power should be transferred to the sovereign and what constraints should there be on the powers of rulers? Locke recognises that a sovereign is a man or collection of men. Just as a man may be unjust to another, so a sovereign could act unjustly. A sovereign may not do as he pleases. The sovereign must do the common good and is answerable to the citizens. While Hobbes believed in a highly authoritarian style of government, with the sovereign holding all the citizens' powers and being able to regulate in all areas of human existence, Locke limits the extent of powers handed over to that which is necessary to achieve the purposes of creating stability and peace and setting up a system of magistrates and courts. Locke preserves human freedom as much as possible and requires the sovereign to perform his duties to the people. The citizen has rights against the state enforceable under the law.

According to Locke, the correct way to understand the sovereign is as a paternalistic, benevolent power. The sovereign must always act to protect the people because that is what the people have consented to. To act more widely is usurpation. A usurper is "where one is got into the possession of what another has right to". The rights trespassed into are not the province of the sovereign but are powers which remain with the citizens. Since the people have not consented to allow the sovereign to act in such areas, the sovereign has no title to act and so no right to expect to be obeyed in these areas. At all times monarchy remains controlled by the consent of the majority of the citizens.

Locke is not merely concerned with the powers and duties of the sovereign but also provides a mythological account of property rights. He tells that natural resources are provided for the use of all. At this stage they are not items of property. However, by harvesting them or adding our labour to them, we may say that we have acquired property in them. Locke writes:

> "He that is nourished by the acorns he picked up under an oak, or the apples he gathered from the trees in the wood, has certainly appropriated them to himself. Nobody can deny but the nourishment is his. I ask, then, when did they begin to be his? When he digested? Or when he ate? Or when he boiled? Or when he brought them home? Or when he picked them up? And it is plain, if the first gathering made them not his, nothing else could. That labour put a distinction between them and common. That added something to them more than Nature, the common mother of all, had done, and so they became his private right."

People have a right to all they have expended their labour upon. This is the foundation of rights of property and is the basis for asserting property when property rights are disputed or encroached upon. But Locke does not think that riches should be limitless. Moderation is required: "a state of liberty is not a state of licence". He writes "it was useless, as well as dishonest, to carve himself too much, or take more than he needed".

Locke's Treatises on Government provide the outlines of a system of limited government, built upon natural rights, rights of individual freedoms and of individual property, limited at all times by the consent of the citizens. The Social Contract involves at its heart the preservation of individual's rights. The rights are exercisable against the Government. They are its reason for existence and its duty to protect. It has no other functions at all.

Locke's thinking has remained very important as a description of a limited or constitutional monarchy. His ideas lie behind the concepts of separation of powers and systems of checks and balances on administrative and legislative acts. More generally, Locke reminds us that the rights of citizens are forms of claim which citizens enjoy only because such rights are recognised in the law of sovereign states, for it is only when rights are recognised in the law that they become enforceable in the courts.

NATURAL AND HUMAN RIGHTS

Classical natural lawyers did not acknowledge the existence of individual rights. Until the 17th century, as we have seen, people thought in terms of duties to monarchs or churches or overlords. Before the 17th century, people used the light of reason to tell them whether a law was good or bad. This enabled them to tell whether the law should be obeyed. Inalienable natural or human rights were an innovation of the 17th and 18th centuries.

The American Constitution of 1776 talked of self-evident truths, that all men are created equal, of people having certain unalienable rights to life, liberty and the pursuit of happiness. The French Declaration of the Rights of Man of 1789 set out 17 fundamental articles.

Even so, it was not until the 20th century that we find clear expressions of human rights. In 1948 the United Nations adopted the Universal Declaration of Human Rights. The Declaration was written in response to the crimes against humanity which occurred in the Second World War. In 1950 the Council of Europe adopted the European Convention on Human Rights and in 1998 the United Kingdom enacted the Human Rights Act which makes certain rights and freedoms derived from the Council of Europe's Convention on Human Rights directly enforceable in United Kingdom law.

As a result, all devolved legislation passed by the Scottish Parliament and all acts of the Scottish Ministers and those who hold powers delegated under them must conform to the Scotland Act 1998 and the Human Rights Act 1998. There have been devolution issues which have raised questions of the competence of actions carried out by the Scottish Ministers. An example of this was an objection to the appointment of temporary sheriffs by the Lord Advocate. Article 6 of the Convention gives a right to "a fair and public hearing within a reasonable time by an independent and impartial tribunal established by law". The sheriffs acted upon the commission of the Lord Advocate who was also responsible for the prosecution of crime. At the end of their temporary term of office, the Lord Advocate could renew their commissions or not. While there was no suggestion that there had ever occurred a conflict of interest, it was submitted in the case of *Starrs* v *Ruxton* (2000) that the public could conceivably think that the Lord Advocate would extend the commissions of only those sheriffs with a good conviction record. Justice had to be seen to be done and so the High Court held that temporary sheriffs were not an independent and impartial tribunal. Today, judges are appointed by a judicial appointments board and the Lord Advocate has no say.

Nevertheless, despite human rights upholding fundamental human values which are used to overrule the operation of national law, it is difficult to see any connection between such rights and the natural law. It is tempting to think that there may be some connections with the ideas of Finnis which we saw in Chapter 2. It will be recalled that Finnis asserted seven basic goods: life, knowledge, play, aesthetic experience, sociability, practical reasonableness, and religion. While there may be some overlap between Finnis's right to life and sociability, the other items in Finnis's descriptive list are of a very different order from the values protected in the Human Rights Act or in any of the other declarations and Conventions on human rights. Finnis himself says that the declarations are based on the need to recognise threats to equality and individual human dignity since political discourse is aimed primarily at achieving the common good. Is it merely contingent that human rights, which serve to overrule or qualify state laws, appear to act like higher law does in the natural law and specifically in being a means of judging human law?

Bentham was very dubious about the status of natural rights. He was of the view that talk of natural rights was meaningless. Bentham criticised Blackstone's natural law and wrote: "Rights is the child of law; from real law come real rights; from imaginary laws, from 'nature', come imaginary rights ... Natural rights is simple nonsense; natural and imprescriptible rights [an American phrase], rhetorical nonsense, nonsense upon stilts."

OVERRIDING OF RIGHTS

While human rights may qualify or overrule national law, there is still a feature which asserts that national law has a higher authority. This is to be found in the overruling of human rights. In the European Convention most of the rights are "qualified" to the effect that individual rights may be withheld where there are good reasons aimed at achieving the common good. Article 8, which asserts a right of respect to privacy and family life, is an example of this. It is heavily qualified. The Article reads:

> "8.1 Everyone has the right to respect for his private and family life, his home and his correspondence. 2. There shall be no interference by a public authority with the exercise of this right except such as is in accordance with the law and is necessary in a democratic society in the interests of national security, public safety or the economic well-being of the country, for the prevention of disorder or crime, for the protection of health and morals, or for the protection of the rights and freedoms of others."

Nor is it simply human rights which are qualified. Other statutory rights are similarly qualified. In the case of *Council of Civil Service Unions* v *Minister for the Civil Service* (1985), national security considerations were used to qualify the right of civil servant unions to strike. Lord Scarman observed:

> "I would dismiss this appeal for one reason only. I am satisfied that the Respondent has made out a case on the basis of national security ... I have no doubt that the respondent refused to consult the unions before issuing the instruction because she feared that, if she did not, union organised disruption of GCHQ monitoring services could well result ... I am satisfied that a reasonable minister could reasonably consider such disruption to constitute a threat to national security ... where a question as to the interests of national security arises in judicial proceedings the court has to act on evidence ... the court will accept the opinion of the crown of its responsible officer."

The bottom line appears to be that national law giveth, and national law taketh away.

DWORKIN AND RIGHTS AS TRUMPS

However, in the United States, the Supreme Court has long had the power to strike down any legislation which appears to contradict fundamental constitutional rights. The same cannot be said in the United Kingdom (although the new Supreme Court has threatened to flex its muscles if the Rule of Law were to be put in issue – though the judges of the Supreme Court have recognised that their decisions, as unelected and appointed officials, do not have the authority of the legislation of the elected House of Commons).

Dworkin, who we saw in Chapter 4, considers the striking down powers of the American Supreme Court in his book *Taking Rights Seriously*, where he describes rights as "trumps". A problem with political policy is that it strives to achieve the common good. This requires a balancing exercise. Dworkin talks of two levels. When considering political policy, deciding upon the common good, it is necessary to consider rights as part of the package involved in a general political theory. At this stage we "must consider what package – what general justification for political decisions together with what right – is most suitable. ... But on other occasions we must take the general theme of some political theory as fixed and consider what rights are necessary as trumps over the general background justification that theory proposes". Even so, Dworkin accepts there may be situations when rights may have to be overridden: "although citizens have a right to free speech, the Government may override that right when necessary to protect the rights of others, or to prevent a catastrophe, or even to obtain a clear and major public benefit".

HOHFELD'S ANALYSIS OF RIGHTS

The most significant view of rights in positive law is that of Wesley Newcomb Hohfeld (1879–1917), an American jurist who produced an important scheme showing how rights can be analysed into their constituent parts and how they are to be understood within a positive law system. Rights talk is often confusing because it confuses different types of rights together when they should be kept separate.

The simple phrase "X has a right" may function differently in different contexts. Hohfeld identified eight different sorts of right and represented them schematically as shown in Figure 8.1.

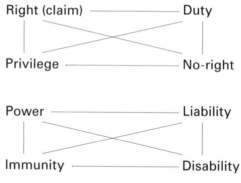

Figure 8.1   Hohfeld's legal relations

In the scheme, the simplest kind of right is a claim to performance, action or forbearance by another person. An example might be X has the right (claim) to be repaid money which is owed to him by Y. This is a simple debt situation. Y is under a duty (obligation) to pay X. This is a simple relation between two persons. For every such claim there is a corresponding duty. Hohfeld uses the term "correlative". A right (in the sense of claim) has a duty as its correlative. We may indeed define a duty as a legal obligation to fulfil the right (claim) of another which, in the event that it is not honoured, may be enforced by legal coercion.

In the second line we find privilege (or liberty) being correlated with no-right. A privilege is a legal freedom in favour of X to conduct himself in a certain manner as he pleases. An example is the right to fish in a river. It follows that there will be a person, Y, who must suffer or allow X to exercise his power (or liberty). Y is correlatively under a no-right. He must allow X to exercise his power. Y has no choice in the matter. He has no right to object if X exercises the power. A privilege therefore has a no-right as its correlative.

In the third line we find power being correlated with liability. A power is the right to create new legal relations (to effect a legal transaction of some sort bringing about new levels of rights and duties) of which Y is the subject. For example, if Y makes an offer to X, X has the power to accept to the offer and hence to bind Y into contractual relations. Y is correlatively under a liability. X may or may not exercise the power but, if X does, then Y is liable to fulfil the offer he has made. Y has no choice in the matter. A power therefore has a liability as its correlative.

An immunity exists where a person, X, is entitled to be freed from any power otherwise held by another person Y. That is to say, X is immune from Y's exercise of his power. In relation to X, Y is under a disability. Y may generally have a power but is disabled from exercising it against X since X has a legal immunity. An immunity therefore has a disability as its correlative.

In the above scheme all correlatives are represented by the horizontal lines.

However, Hohfeld also uses his diagram to represent other sorts of connection. The diagonals involve opposites. The opposite of a right (claim) is where there is no right. That much is obvious. It is less than obvious that the opposite of a privilege is a duty, that the opposite of a power is a disability, and that the opposite of an immunity is a liability. But, on fine analysis, you will see that this is so. A power, for example, is where a person has the ability to create new legal relations over another who is liable to suffer them. A disability is where such a power is utterly frustrated. The importance of opposites is that where one of them exists, the other must be excluded. Where a person, X, has a right (claim) against Y, then the same person X cannot have no-right against Y in the same subject-matter. A right and a no-right are opposites. Similarly, when X has a privilege against Y, X cannot have a duty in relation to Y regarding the same subject-matter.

In this way Hohfeld has created a scheme which he considers analyses all the sorts of rights and obligations which are to be found in the law. Our problem is that we use the term "right" loosely. We should be precise. We fall into error if we are not. The force of the diagram is that we have here a sort of truth function table for understanding the logical relations inherent in the talk of rights. In every case we are dealing with bilateral relations. For every X, there is a Y.

Hohfeld's analysis is important but there are problems with it, some of which will be dealt with in the next section. Hohfeld thought he had clarified some ambiguities of the use of rights talk. In his own words, he says "in any closely-reasoned problem, whether legal or non-legal, chameleon-hued words are a peril both to clear thought and lucid expression". It is not so clear that he has achieved his aim.

MacCORMICK'S CRITICISM OF HOHFELD

In *Institutions of Law* MacCormick criticises Hohfeld's theory of rights. MacCormick thinks that while Hohfeld's analysis covers a wide range of ways in which we use rights talk within the civil law, the analysis is nonetheless incomplete. In particular, Hohfeld fails to take proper account of choices and interests.

That rights involve choices was a matter considered by H L A Hart who put forward what has come to be known as the Choice or Will theory of rights. Hart thought that rights are created by legal rules and it makes no sense to talk about them except by reference to the legal rule concerned. The rule will explain the right in terms of Hohfeld's right–duty correlation. But the right holder always has the choice as to whether or not to exercise the right. Hence it follows that the exact nature of the person under obligation depends on the right holder's choice whether to exercise/enforce or not.

Similarly, rights may involve separate interests. This was a matter considered by Dworkin, who made a distinction among right-based, duty-based, and goal-based interests. This is discussed very clearly in Jeremy Waldron's *Theories of Rights*. Waldron gives the example of torture. He says that a prohibition of torture is right based where an objection is motivated by concern for the individual suffering victim. The objection is duty based where an objection is motivated by concern that the torturer, being forced to torture as a matter of duty, may feel degraded by performing the duty to torture. An objection is goal based where it is generated by a concern for the effect of the torture on society as a whole. Rights under this analysis may involve any or all of these separate interests.

MacCormick's objection is that rights can occur which do not involve choices for the rights holder. But choices concerning the right may be exercised by a third party who has an interest in the right. Hohfeld's analysis is far too simple to be able to analyse this situation.

MacCormick illustrates this by reference to the situation where a minor child has suffered injury through (say) medical negligence. The law recognises that the child is entitled to damages for the loss and injury suffered. So there is an operative legal rule. However, the child lacks legal capacity to take remedial action and sue for damages. In these circumstances, some person with capacity, such as a parent or guardian, may be given, as a result of another rule of law, the right to act on behalf of the child and to pursue the child's claim for damages. It should be noted that in this scenario the child has a right recognised by law but has no choice as to whether or not it is exercised. This disproves Hart's analysis of choices. It should also be noted that the parent or guardian has a legal interest in the child's right. It is a matter of choice for the parent whether or not to pursue damages on the child's behalf. If successful the parent will hold the funds in a trust on the child's behalf.

But this is not yet the end of the story. The parent looking after such a child needs to provide an appropriate level of services and support for the child, and to do so may require special adaptations to their home and also special equipment. This may entitle the parents to damages for their additional expenses. The parent may therefore have yet a separate right of action against the negligent party for damages in relation to these matters too.

MacCormick's scenario may be complex but it is regrettably not at all unusual. A proper analysis of rights should be capable of showing how these additional elements of choice and interest fit in. Hohfeld's analysis is simply not sensitive enough to do so.

Another feature of Hohfeld's analysis is that it is concerned with simple bilateral positions. For every kind of right there is a single party under a definite type of obligation. Clearly, Hohfeld has only civil rights in mind. But this is not the only kind of right there is. MacCormick is also concerned with rights arising in connection with criminal law: rights not to be assaulted, for example.

MacCormick therefore makes a distinction between active and passive rights. An active right is a right to exercise choice whether or not to *do* something. MacCormick substitutes "v" for the verb. An active right is a right to v or a right not to v. It is in the discretion of the right holder whether or not to exercise the right concerned. Being or acting within one's rights pertains to active rights. Passive rights are rights to be treated in a certain way by people in general. MacCormick says that "essential to the existence of every passive right ("claim-right') is either a prior or a resultant requirement on classes or individuals to act or abstain in favour of persons who hold such a right". That is to say, it is the right not to have someone *v* against one, or alternatively the right to expect people to *v* in relation to one. Using the assault example, we have the right to expect to be able to go about without being assaulted by other citizens. The crime of assault correlates with such an expectation. Passive rights therefore may well involve expectations concerning the behaviour of groups or individuals or even of everyone else in society other than the right holder. Again, we find that Hohfeld's analysis, being concerned with simple bilateral relations only, is really not sensitive to such issues.

Essential concepts

- Roman law recognises persons and the legal relationships they have with others. Relationships could be created voluntary by contracts with other citizens or involuntarily as a result of a harm being done by one citizen against another.

- There are positive rights and negative rights; private rights and public rights; perfect rights and imperfect rights; primary rights and secondary rights (or accessory rights); rights *in personam* and rights *ad rem*.

- For Locke, the natural state of mankind is not "nasty" and "brutish". It was a state of perfect freedom for individuals. It was a state of equality. There was peace rather than war. Even in a state of nature, one person was not permitted to harm another.

- After the Social Contract the sovereign holds the power of the community. The sovereign owes duties to citizens and is required to defend citizens by putting magistrates in place to punish those who harm individuals and to order reparation. The state must also protect the peace and preserve the life, health, liberty and possessions of the citizens.

- Locke limits the extent of powers handed over to that which is necessary to achieve the purposes of creating stability and peace and setting up a system of magistrates and courts. Locke preserves human freedom as much as possible and requires the sovereign to perform his duties to the people. The citizen has rights against the state enforceable under the law.

- The sovereign must always act to protect the people because that is what the people have consented to. To act more widely is usurpation. Since the people have not consented to allow the sovereign to act in such areas, the sovereign has no title to act and so no right to expect to be obeyed in these areas. At all times monarchy remains controlled by the consent of the majority of the citizens.

- People have a right to all they have expended their labour upon. This is the foundation of rights of property and is the basis for asserting property when property rights are disputed or encroached upon. But Locke does not think that riches should be limitless.

- Locke's thinking has remained very important as a description of a limited or constitutional monarchy. His ideas lie behind the concepts of separation of powers and systems of checks and balances on administrative and legislative acts.

- Classical natural lawyers did not acknowledge the existence of individual rights. Until the 17th century, people thought in terms of duties to monarchs or churches or overlords.

- Inalienable natural or human rights were an innovation of the 17th and 18th centuries, as in the US Declaration of Independence of 1776 and the French Declaration of the Rights of Man of 1789.

- The Human Rights Act 1998 makes certain rights and freedoms, derived from the Council of Europe's Convention on Human Rights, directly enforceable in United Kingdom law.

- The powers of the Scottish Parliament and Scottish Ministers must conform to the Scotland Act 1998 and the Human Rights Act 1998. In *Starrs* v *Ruxton* (2000) the High Court held that temporary sheriffs were not an independent and impartial tribunal as required under Art 6.

- Bentham thought that talk of natural rights was meaningless nonsense.

- In the European Convention most of the human rights are "qualified" and may be overridden where there are good reasons aimed at achieving the common good. In the case of *Council of Civil Service Unions* v *Minister for the Civil Service* (1985), national security considerations were used to qualify and so override the right of civil servant unions to strike.

- Dworkin describes rights as "trumps". When considering political policy, deciding upon the common good, it is necessary to consider rights as part of the package involved in a general political theory. On other occasions we must take the general theme of some political theory as fixed and consider what rights are necessary as trumps over the general background justification that theory proposes.

- Hohfeld produced an important scheme showing how rights should be analysed. Rights talk is often confusing because it confuses different types of rights together when they should be kept separate.
- The scheme has correlatives and opposites. Correlatives go together. Where X holds one type of right, Y is under the correlative. In the scheme, rights (claims) correlate with duties; privileges correlate with "no-rights'; powers correlate with liabilities; and immunities correlate with disabilities.
- Hart says that rights are only explicable by reference to a rule of law and that there must always be a choice as to whether or not to exercise them. This is called the Choice theory.
- Dworkin and Waldron make a distinction among right-based, duty-based, and goal-based interests. Waldron gives the example of torture. There may be several interests contingently existing in relation to one instance of a right. This is called the Interest theory.
- MacCormick analyses a situation where a child is entitled to reparation owed as reparation for an act of medical negligence. The law recognises the child's interest. The child has the right but is not able exercise the right. The law may also make provision for a parent or guardian to act on behalf of the child. The parent has the choice as to whether to exercise or enforce the child's right. In addition the parent may have a separate interest to sue for damages for their own losses. Hohfeld's analysis is simply not sensitive to such differences of choice or interest.
- MacCormick distinguishes between active and passive rights. An active right is a right to exercise choice whether to do something. Passive rights are rights to be treated in a certain way by people in general. We have the right to expect to be able to go about without being assaulted by other citizens. Passive rights therefore may well involve expectations of groups or individuals or even of everyone else in society. Hohfeld's analysis, being concerned with bilateral civil law relations only, is really not sensitive to passive rights.

9 JUSTICE

From an early age we are aware of the idea of justice. Children sharing a birthday cake with friends will all want to get an equally sized slice. No-one should get a bigger slice than anyone else. To allow that would be unfair. Fairness seems to demand that people should be treated equally. Everyone should have a share in whatever good things fall to be distributed and equally everyone should bear a share of any burdens which need to be borne. Distribution seems to involve something amounting to Utilitarian principles. Justice does involve issues of this sort but it includes other ideas too. Sometimes it seems to involve doing what is right. Here we may look to natural law principles. We shall look at the development of some of these ideas in the work of Plato and Aristotle and thereafter we shall compare and contrast the ideas of Rawls and Nozick.

PLATO

Plato, in the *Republic* saw justice as being an attribute of the state. Plato's view of the state was authoritarian and rather repugnant to us today. Nevertheless it was based on the necessities of his era. The role of the legislator was to take charge of all his citizens, from the cradle to the grave, to control them by administering punishments and rewards, to teach them what is right and wrong in every aspect of life, and to impose justice in all their contracts and dealings and in the way they spend their money. Plato did not believe in equality either. He argued that people were basically unequal. The state was made up of many different people with different attributes. In the division of labour which made up the state, some people would be naturally fitted for some tasks and others to other tasks. The demands of an ancient Greek state meant that it required soldiers, craftsmen and rulers. The existence and threat of wars would give rise to a warrior class. The best soldiers would be those who had natural courage. Some people had the attribute of wisdom and these should be the rulers of the state. The other people should be craftsmen. Therefore there would be three classes: a ruling aristocracy, the guardian warriors and craftsmen. Plato likened them respectively to gold, silver and bronze metal. Justice comprised the fulfilling by the people of their roles for the state. And since they had those roles because of their personal attributes, it follows that they were at the same time using their individual abilities to the full. Plato thought this would give rise to a just state where harmony and contentment would be brought into being, with reason being at its head.

However, the perfect state could suffer from degeneration if people sought their own personal desires rather than seeking the common good. There were five different types of state. One was the ideal state and the other four were different sorts of degenerate state that were possible depending on the type of failure that occurred in their rulers:

(1) The ideal state was run by philosopher rulers who would rule with wisdom and impose reason. This form of state would be harmonious.

(2) If rulers sought personal ambition and lusted after honour the ideal state would degenerate into a timocracy.

(3) Further degeneration produces a plutocracy in which power would be seized and held by a small number who sought after power and wealth. In this sort of state the rich would rise to power and the virtuous would sink into obscurity.

(4) The next stage of degeneration would produce democracy in which the ruling is done by people with no particular ability or training to rule. Such a state would show a very low level of justice and so produce antagonisms.

(5) The lowest level of degeneration would be despotism where a single despot takes power and enslaves the people for his own ends. The despot is the "enlargement of the unjust soul" with a master passion overruling justice completely.

The ideal state was also described in Plato's late writing, the *Laws*. Here, Plato describes how the legislator causes people to achieve a righteous life by means of educative laws, minutely detailed and rigidly enforced, based upon absolute standards of morality and total obedience during all of their lives. These laws were aimed at achieving three ends:

(1) Modest standards of living would be encouraged, avoiding excesses that could destroy social harmony.

(2) Each family within the state (the state would be limited to a total population of 5,040) will own a farm, but manual labour would be performed by slaves, and trade would be carried out by resident foreigners.

(3) Education would fit citizens for the occupations that suited their attributes. However all men and women would be taught to fight so that they could defend the state.

In these ways, Plato's idea of "justice" was very different from today's ideas. The word Plato uses for justice is "dikaiosune" which means "righteousness" or "virtue". In essence it is aimed at causing citizens make the best of their abilities and thereby they would each add to the common good. But at the same time individual attributes causes there to be a rigid class system approved and encouraged by the laws. The state not only guides the individual but has the power to interfere in every aspect of life. There are in principle no areas of life that the state could not legislate within. Plato did not appear to have any concept of individual freedom.

ARISTOTLE

Aristotle set out to describe how law should operate. Aristotle saw the state, the law giver and governor, as fitting the individual citizen for the good life and satisfying his social instincts. But problems arose from the administration of law. Law's purpose was to rule but it could be abused by an autocrat because the law offers the means of attaining the autocrat's personal wishes. Any rule by one person is likely to suffer from defects caused by the ruler's appetites and high spirit. Rule by God and by reason would be best. A good law maker would operate reason free from passions. Since laws should rule the lives of all citizens, there is another danger: that of rigidity. Laws are general rules but are imposed in a variety of situations many of which the law maker could not have had in contemplation. This could result in injustice when imposed in some situations. Justice could be achieved by means of the concept of equity. Equity would apply the spirit rather than the letter of the rule. By this means the oversimplifications of the law maker would be corrected, and the over- universalisation of rules avoided. Equity would also act to pardon individuals for their human failings. Aristotle writes:

> "When, therefore, the law lays down a general rule, and thereafter a case arises falling outside the general model, it is then right, where the lawyer's words have turned out to be too simple to meet the case without doing wrong, to rectify the deficiency by deciding as the law-giver would himself decide if he were present on the occasion and would have enacted if he were aware of the case in question." [the Nichomachean Ethics]

And again: "it is equity to pardon the human failing, to look to the law-giver and not to the law, to the spirit and not to the action" [the Rhetoric]. Justice, therefore, is to be found within the process of law by means of reason and equity. These concepts are still major components of justice in the law today.

Two further concepts are found in Aristotle's works. These are the concepts of distributive and corrective justice. Distributive justice has to do with the distribution of honour and wealth and all other divisible assets of the community. Aristotle says these may be shared equally or not since equals should be treated equally and unequals unequally. Aristotle's society, like that of Plato, was not an equal society. Justice, however, aims at proper proportion in contrast to disproportion which characterises injustice. Corrective justice is concerned with the restoration of a disturbed equilibrium. A judge will treat parties as equals, will discover what harm has been committed and will seek to equalise the situation. The judge will impose penalties on those who have received ill gotten gains and in so doing will restore the parties to their previous position, and recompense those who have suffered. Corrective justice involves both civil and criminal matters for justice will be imposed in voluntary transactions (such as selling, buying, hiring, lending and pledging) and in involuntary transactions (such as theft, assault and maiming).

Aristotle's ideas of reason, universalised laws, equity, and distributive and corrective justice provide much of the foundation of our modern idea of justice.

MILL'S UTILITARIANISM AND JUSTICE

There is a strong connection between distributive justice and Utilitarianism. Aristotle's sharing out of goods required to be proportionate but not equal. Utilitarianism provides a formula for the distribution of goods among a society on the basis of "the greatest good for the greatest number". This would also apply to the distribution of evils. But there are problems with interpreting the Utilitarian formula. These were addressed by John Stuart Mill, who made an interesting contribution to justice and equity. Mill wrote that "the happiness which forms the utilitarian standard of what is right in conduct is not the agent's own happiness but that of all concerned. ... In the golden rule of Jesus, we read the complete spirit of the ethics of utility. To do as one would be done by, and to love one's neighbour as oneself, constitute the ideal of utilitarian perfection".

In translating these ideas into legal practices, Mill says that "laws and social arrangements should place the interest of every individual as nearly as possible in harmony with the interest of the whole; and secondly that education and opinion ... shall so use that power ... that a direct impulse to promote the general good may be in every individual one of the habitual motives of action".

Justice involves not only doing the right thing, but also avoiding doing the wrong thing. Rules apply equally to all the people to whom the rules are addressed. Rules are aimed at producing the common good. People who break rules should be punished. But justice in civil cases is based on retaliation when harmed. When a person's rights are violated or a person is harmed, the court should take action. No action should arise if no harm has been done. Justice therefore involves moral concepts. It moves beyond mere utility and becomes grounds for sympathy and self-interest. Other moral issues arise, such as that of individual liberty. In the balance of interests between the individual and the state, there should be limits to the right of a Government to interfere with an individual's interests. The state has no right to interfere with an individual's choices when dealing purely with the individual's own interests. Thus an individual has the right of freedom of expression and the state has no right to silence his opinion. Mill has expanded away from Utilitarian calculations and developed new moral aspects of justice in the forms of the harm principle, individual liberty and freedom of expression and opinion. These concepts are complex to evaluate and states still find it difficult to reach a balance where issues of individual liberty and freedom of expression are concerned.

RAWLS, NOZICK AND SOCIAL JUSTICE

John Rawls and Robert Nozick both wrote about social justice. Rawls was in favour of progressive taxes to redistribute wealth away from the rich and benefit the poor by means of welfare provision, while Nozick opposed taxation and thought that welfare provision should be in private hands. There is also an allied problem of how much state there should be. Nozick was in favour only of a minimal state.

Rawls

In *A Theory of Justice* Rawls puts forward his ideas about social justice. Utilitarianism is unable to evaluate social justice because it cannot clearly differentiate between the common good and the individual. Unfairness occurs when one group in society increases in happiness while another group suffers a corresponding reduction in happiness. A Utilitarian calculus is not sensitive to this situation. A proper system of social justice would also look not merely at wealth and assets but also at social goods such as self-respect. Free and rational persons should be able to choose the basic structure of society so that it will produce the maximum fairness. How can this be achieved? Modern societies already have particular forms of government and political and economic structures. It seems that to create a fair society we should start from scratch, which is impossible. As a result Rawls embarks on a thought experiment.

Rawls imagines a kind of social contract intended not to create a form of government but rather to create principles of justice aimed at producing a fair society. A social contract requires citizens. These people would have to start from an original position. Rawls imagines that "people in the original position" would have to start as equals. They will each differ in terms of sex, religion, physical strength and social position. But for the purposes of debating and deciding upon the principles of justice, to avoid self-interest, they should not know what sex, religion, physical strength and social position they have. They should also not know what role or social position they will eventually acquire in the society whose principles of justice they are to choose. Rawls says they should therefore be under a "veil of ignorance". From under this veil of ignorance, the people must now debate and unanimously agree a set of principles that will give them the best chance of a good life. As no individual knows how advantaged or disadvantaged they will finally be, they will all tend to avoid choosing principles which will make life intolerable for the poorest and most disadvantaged member in society. No person who acknowledges the risk that they might become that poorest and most disadvantaged person would wish that person's life to be intolerable. Instead they will opt for a system in which there will at the very least be a basic measure of welfare provision for the poorest people. They would choose principles of justice having the general benefit for society in mind. They would choose general rules which would avoid giving unfair advantage to some at the expense of others. Rawls supports his ideas by using what he calls a "maximin" table. This is a table which shows ranges of decisions and outcomes in quantifiable terms. In this way the people would choose principles which would produce the least disadvantageous outcome for the poorest and most disadvantaged of them in the new society. In a sense this is simply a form of potential self-preservation.

Rawls concludes that the people under the veil of ignorance would choose two principles of justice. First, each person is to have an equal right to the most extensive total system of equal basic liberties compatible with a similar system of liberty for all. Second, social and economic equalities are to be arranged so that they are both (a) to the greatest benefit of the least advantaged, consistent with the just savings principle, and (b) attached to offices and positions open to all under conditions of fair equality of opportunity. These principles need some explanation. The first principle is about liberties, while the second is about equalities. Liberties have to be satisfied before equalities. The first principle decides the level of liberties which people are equally entitled to. The liberties are such things as the right to vote, eligibility for public office, freedom of speech, thought, expression, assembly, freedom of the person, the right to hold property, freedom from arbitrary arrest, and so on. Rawls thinks that people will choose a high level of liberties. The second principle ensures that the least advantaged will gain a reasonable level of benefits. The distribution of benefits does not require to be done equally. But where some people become entitled to greater benefits, there should be no injustice to those who do not become so entitled provided that at the same time they should attain some level of improvement. There is also no harm in some people benefitting socially and economically from offices and positions provided that there are fair and equal opportunities of access to those offices and positions. Rawls's thought experiment has a number of weaknesses not least that the scenario is wholly hypothetical and could never happen in the real world. Nozick puts forward a devastating attack to which we now turn.

Nozick

Nozick was a pupil of Rawls but objected to the idea that the state should use progressive taxation to achieve a redistribution of wealth. Nozick believed that a just society depends upon individualism. Each individual is free and has inalienable natural rights which are limited only by the need to recognise the reciprocal rights of others. Forced redistribution of wealth contradicts individual autonomy. Nozick says that benefits can be acquired legitimately in three ways:

(1) by the "principle of acquisition" in which property hitherto un-owned is acquired in a just way (usually when a person expends his labour on making or improving a resource);

(2) by the "principle of transfer" in which the ownership of property passes from one person to another in accordance with just principles; and

(3) by the "principle of justice in rectification" which states that no-one is entitled to hold any benefit except where this comes about as a result of some combination of the first and second principles.

Nozick builds his system by adopting certain arguments about the right of property ownership first proposed by Locke and which support the principle of acquisition. The arguments Nozick uses to support the principle of acquisition are sometimes termed the "self-ownership argument" and the "creation without wrong" argument.

First, the self-ownership argument has four steps:

(1) if I am not a slave, nobody owns my body. Therefore:
(2) I must own myself;
(3) if I own myself then I must own all of my actions, including those that create or improve resources; Therefore:
(4) I own the resources or the improvements I produce.

Using this argument Nozick concludes that any redistributive taxation, whereby the state takes property from one individual to give to another, is tantamount to slavery or forced labour. That is to say that if the state takes a share of my property, then the state has forcibly taken a share of the labour I have expended, and so has forcibly taken advantage of my actions. It is this that is equivalent to slavery.

Second, the creation without wrong argument has three steps:

(1) if a person creates a new item of social wealth; and
(2) wrongs no-one in doing so; it follows that
(3) he ought to be accorded ownership of the item.

Only when wealth created does not make others worse off can the process be regarded as just. It is perfectly legitimate for people to acquire wealth justly. And if they do so then they should be entitled to hold on to their wealth – even if others in the same society are not wealthy.

Of course these arguments are partly rhetorical devices to highlight Nozick's repugnance to Rawls's liberal thinking. Nozick believed in a free market with no intervention by the state. The state's only proper functions are the protection of internal and external security and the administration of justice through the courts. Nozick believes in a minimal state. Rawls's theory makes the state the provider of welfare, health and education. Nozick thinks that these social goods should not be provided by the state but by private organisations. His reasons are that private organisations will compete with each other and strive to be efficient. This will ensure high-quality services at reasonable cost. States, however, have no-one to compete with and history shows that they are inefficient. States also do not give due regard to individual rights. It is for these reasons that states should be minimal.

So far as redistribution of wealth is concerned, Nozick does not believe that there could be a central redistributing agency. But even if this could be achieved, the state of equality produced thereby would be only temporary. Individuals have different abilities and those who had wealth before would soon gain new wealth through their enterprise, while those who were poor before would return to that state.

There are difficulties with Nozick's approach. His theory is based on little supporting data and relies on rhetorical arguments. Some have asked whether a state can exist in a minimal form. How is it to be kept minimal? How can those in positions of political power be prevented from acquiring more power?

Rawls and Nozick present two very opposing views about the role of the state in ensuring social justice – a fair distribution of social goods. This is a very specific role that all modern states now undertake to a greater or lesser degree. While this involves an understanding of justice, it is clear that this notion of justice is very different in character from the notions of legal justice which we examined in the earlier sections of this chapter.

Essential concepts

- For Plato, the role of the legislator was to take charge of all his citizens by administering punishments and rewards, to teach them what is right and wrong and to impose justice in all their contracts and dealings and in the way they spend their money.
- Plato argued that people were basically unequal.
- In the ideal state, there would be three classes: a ruling aristocracy, guardian warriors and craftsmen. Plato likened them respectively to gold, silver and bronze metal.
- However, the perfect state could suffer from degeneration if people sought their own personal desires rather than seeking the common good.
- The ideal state could degenerate into timocracy, plutarchy, democracy or despotism. This would occur where the rulers ceased to govern rationally and virtuously and so failed to pursue the common good.

- Plato defines justice as "righteousness" or "virtue". In essence it is aimed at causing citizens make the best of their abilities and thereby they would each add to the common good.

Aristotle

- A good law maker would operate reason free from passions.
- Laws are general rules but are imposed in a variety of situations many of which the law maker could not have had in contemplation. This could result in injustice. Justice could be achieved by means of the concept of equity.
- Equity would apply the spirit rather than the letter of the rule. Equity would also act to pardon individuals for their human failings.
- Distributive justice has to do with the distribution of honour and wealth and all other divisible assets of the community. Justice aims at proper proportion in contrast to disproportion which characterises injustice.
- Corrective justice is concerned with the restoration of a disturbed equilibrium. A judge will treat parties as equals, will discover what harm has been committed and will impose penalties on wrongdoers while compensating those who have suffered.

Mill

- Justice is based on retaliation when harmed. When a person's rights are violated or a person is harmed, the court should take action. No action should arise if no harm has been done.
- Justice involves moral concepts. It includes individual liberty. A Government should not interfere with an individual's choices when dealing only with the individual's own interests.
- An individual has the right of freedom of expression and the state has no right to silence his opinion.

Rawls

- Unfairness occurs when one group in society increases in happiness while another group suffers a corresponding reduction in happiness. A Utilitarian calculus is not sensitive to this situation.
- Rawls imagines a "people in the original position" as equals. They will each differ in terms of sex, religion, physical strength and social

position. But they should be under a "veil of ignorance" as to their differences.

- The people will agree a set of principles that will give them the best chance of a good life. They will choose a basic measure of welfare provision for the poorest people. They will choose a system of liberties for all and equality of opportunities and benefits.

Nozick

- Nozick believed that a just society depends upon individualism. Each individual is free and has inalienable natural rights which are limited only by the need to recognise the reciprocal rights of others.
- Property can be acquired legitimately by expending labour, by receiving property as a gift, or by some combination of these two. Redistributive taxation is tantamount to slavery or forced labour. Nozick believed in a free market with no intervention by the state.
- The state should be minimal. It should be concerned with internal and external security and with legal administration through the courts. It is not the business of the state to provide welfare, health or education.
- Social goods are more efficiently provided by private organisations which strive for efficiency.
- States are inefficient service providers and do not give due regard to individual rights.

10 THE JUSTIFICATION OF PUNISHMENT

Punishment is the element of sanction imposed on a person who has broken the criminal law. When offences are enacted, the enacting statutes tend to indicate the level of punishment by reference to a standard scale of fine or length of prison term. This is not the case for common law crimes. The general practice is that the more serious the crime, the greater should be the level of punishment. However, the judge has discretion in setting an appropriate punishment and has to take into account a range of factors including the seriousness and results of the crime and any mitigating factors, whether a discount should be given for pleading guilty, whether the accused has previous convictions, the circumstances of the accused (for example, learning difficulties suffered, drug or alcohol addiction, anger management problems), the suitability of an accused for particular disposals such as probation, community service, etc.

Punishment is so well established an institution that it may seem that it is unquestionably justified. However, punishment is the imposition of coercion by the state and surely that fact does require justification in terms of its purposes. There are roughly two main ways of looking at punishment: first, the retributive view which states that a punishment is deserved on moral grounds and that the amount of punishment deserved depends on the seriousness of the original crime; and second, the Utilitarian view which justifies punishment on the basis that it will bring about a better future – often in terms of deterrence, rehabilitation or cure.

RETRIBUTIVE THEORIES

Retributive theories take a simple moral view that the criminal, in committing a crime, has done an evil to the victim, which harm can only be healed by the criminal himself suffering a harm which is equal and opposite in moral seriousness. The measure of punishment therefore involves an essentially backwards look in time to assess the quantum of moral evil which the criminal has committed. From this view, we learn that criminals deserve punishment and that the punishment they get should fit the crime. We feel that in suffering the punishment, the criminal is in some way paying the appropriate and deserved penalty for the crime. Such a view is very ancient.

The earliest extant legal code is that of the Babylonian King Hammurabi whose code is some 4,000 years old. The code was written so that the elders of a community, acting on the King's behalf, could administer the King's justice with as much effect in one part of the kingdom as in any other. The populace would take notice of the code and would therefore know what was expected of them. The code includes civil as well as criminal laws. And for every crime identified there was an associated punishment to be meted out to the wrongdoer. Punishments are scaled in accordance with the seriousness of the crime and also the social standing of the criminal and social importance of the harm (for example crimes against the gods or the King are more serious than those against individual citizens). Some punishments are expressed as directly proportional to the harm originally done. For example, Art 8, which deals with theft, states: "If any one steal cattle or sheep, or an ass, or a pig or a goat, if it belong to a god or to the court, the thief shall pay thirtyfold; if it belonged to a freed man of the king he shall pay tenfold; if the thief has nothing with which to pay he shall be put to death." As a result of the Code, the reign of King Hammurabi is recorded as being politically stable, peaceful and just and Hammurabi is described in the code as being "like a real father to his people and ... [who] established prosperity ... and (gave) good government to the land".

Another early formulation of a retributive rule is the Biblical *lex talionis* (literally, the law of retaliation: "an eye for an eye and a tooth for a tooth, an arm for an arm, a life for a life") which is to be found in the Old Testament book of *Leviticus* 24.19–21. This law justified retaliation up to but not beyond the level of the harm done. In this way satisfaction could be obtained by the victim of the harm and so scores were settled and would not give rise to family feuds. It follows that an important part of any retributive system is that people within society should be satisfied that an appropriate level of punishment has been inflicted and will be extracted. Even today, there is a public outcry where a punishment is considered too lenient for the crime which has been perpetrated.

Some recent thinkers have suggested that the idea of equal and opposite punishment should be enforced with more rigour so that the crime of murder should involve the criminal's own life being forfeit, a theft of property should involve the criminal losing his own property, an assault should be responded to with corporal punishment upon the criminal, etc. There are indications in Kelsen's writings that this is the way he thought that forms of punishment were justified. However, in practice such a view is far from satisfactory. It is difficult to apply this to crimes such as rape, fraud, and so on. In any event in contemporary Scotland the death penalty and corporal punishments have been abolished.

There are two different approaches to retributive punishment. Strong retributivists argue that it is enough to punish a deserving criminal with a punishment that fits his crime. Morality is satisfied. Nothing else is required. Robert Nozick considers that punishment is an act of "communicative behaviour" which communicates the wrongness and seriousness of the crime to the criminal in language that he can understand. Weak retributivists, however, argue that a criminal must not only deserve to be punished but that the punishment should additionally produce beneficial effects such as deterrence. Moral justification is not enough. For both types of retributivism, the punishment must be deserved. This is an important point to which we will return.

While, originally, retributivism may have been part of a religious idea, namely that vengeance belonged to God, it is still appropriate, in the interests of justice, for an ordered society to impose a punishment though this is no longer seen as a form of vengeance. Such a system of moral cause and effect can be seen as providing for the moral and possibly psychological needs of the victim, society (and perhaps also for the culprit – for once the penalty is paid, he may regard himself in a sense as redeemed and free once more to go about his way in society without fear of further vengeance). It can also be argued that a role of punishment is to provide a counterbalance to the pleasure that commission of the crime produces for the criminal. Only if the criminal comes to recognise that a decision to commit the crime brings the certainty of future pains as well will the criminal be able in the future to make a proper choice, for only then will the whole effects of the crime be made clear to him. As against these positive arguments, critics may argue that a retributive view of punishment is essentially one of vengeance and that it is therefore barbaric, uncivilised and essentially inconsistent with contemporary values.

UTILITARIAN THEORIES

Utilitarians, being consequentialists, analyse things very differently. They are essentially forward looking and seek the justification for punishment in the ability that a punishment has to produce future good effects and reduce future harms.

Bentham, the author of Utilitarianism, concentrated on the idea of pleasure and pains as being the motive for our actions. He objected to the excessive nature of some of the punishment regimes imposed in the

18th century. He was concerned that after a crime has been committed it immediately strikes us that to inflict a punishment increases the total amount of pain and suffering in the whole system. This fact demands that punishment as an institution requires justification. But such justification is readily to be found. Bentham considered that the principle role for punishment is to discourage a criminal from future criminal behaviour. Clearly, a punishment will fulfil this role if it is severe enough to deter the criminal from committing future crimes. A greater amount of severity is redundant. If it deters others too then that is an additional benefit. Bentham spent much time devising ways of rational punishment. One of his ideas was for a Panopticon – a type of prison in which a criminal could be kept under surveillance at all times. A work regime, the treadmill, ensured that prisoners came to recognise the severity of what they had done. This was thought to be morally improving.

Under the Utilitarian banner we find a number of related consequentialist justifications: deterrence, rehabilitation, therapy and social theories of punishment. Rehabilitation is aimed at enabling a criminal to recognise the harm that their criminal behaviour creates and to getting him to recognise the error of his ways, to avoid forms of criminal behaviour, and learn new forms of behaviour. This may be achieved by the learning of a trade or by other forms of education. Therapeutic approaches regard criminal behaviour as an expression of an aberrant character and so they attempt to address the defects in the criminal's character. These may involve drug and alcohol addiction rehabilitation programmes, anger management programmes, aversion and other psychological therapies. Social theories look at ways of appeasing society for the moral outrage that crimes create. Some social theories are much more radical and may regard the issue of punishment of an offender as secondary. Perhaps it is society that is sick? Criminals may be simply reacting in predictable ways to social and educational deprivation or the lack of opportunities for advancement. The cure for these is to give the criminal education and employment training while at the same time campaigning for a general improvement in society as a whole.

Utilitarian justifications for punishment have some well-known difficulties. We saw earlier that Consequentialist moral theories suffer from some well known problems. A particular difficulty arises with the idea that "the end justifies the means". A criminal may be deterred from continuing his criminal behaviour by the imposition of suitable punishment. But deterrence may be equally effective where the persons punished have not committed the crime at all. A member of the criminal's family or someone known to him may be punished instead. The Romans quelled uprisings by the practice of "decimation" which involved lining up rebellious citizens and executing every tenth one of them. This had a strong deterrent effect on those remaining. So the concept of deserts, which was essential to any retributive theory of punishment, has no such necessary involvement in a Utilitarian theory. And there are other problems too. When looking at a rehabilitative or therapeutic punishment, the amount of the punishment will be effective only when the person has become rehabilitated or cured of their aberrant behaviour. Until that time they should remain incarcerated – indefinitely, forever if need be. And who is to say when that rehabilitation or cure has occurred – presumably only on the say-so of a psychologist or other technical or medical specialist? These problems were described in a famous passage by C S Lewis in "The Humanitarian Theory of Punishment" which stresses the importance of the idea of just deserts. The article is well worth seeking out and reading.

KELSEN AND THE CAUSAL NECESSITY OF PUNISHMENT

We saw earlier that Kelsen's Pure Theory involved a causal approach to a law. A law is a norm addressed to the individual citizen and requires him to do or forbear from doing a particular piece of behaviour. But at the same time the law is addressed to an official and obliges him, in the event that the law is breached by the citizen, to impose the relative sanction. Kelsen describes such norms as having causal efficacy: if X then Y; if not-Y then Z. The advantages of this approach are two-fold. First, the purpose of the norm is taken seriously. The level of sanction attached to the norm is a clear intimation to the citizen of the importance of underlying values and of compliance with the norm. Second, the citizen is given notice of what will happen to him if he chooses to disobey the norm. Such transparency gives the citizen an opportunity to orientate his actions with the expectations of the state. An ideal and transparent system of law will fulfil both these two objectives. Unfortunately, few modern states have taken the opportunity to express criminal codes with such clarity. But the German criminal code would appear to be an apt example. For each crime, the punishment is clearly indicated. And what of the measure of punishment? Such a system does enable a state to review the efficacy of its laws on a regular basis. If there are too many incidents of one particular crime then the punishment level may be increased, with a correlating increase in deterrent effect. In this way a scientific method of punishment can be built up.

While in the United Kingdom we do not have such a system, stating the amount of punishment for a crime does have the benefit of giving a clear indication to the citizens of the seriousness of criminal behaviour. This parallels to some extent Nozick's idea of "communicative behaviour" to which we have already referred.

FOUCAULT AND THE DECONSTRUCTION OF PUNISHMENT

We saw earlier that Critical Legal Studies theorists and Postmodern theorists deconstruct laws to show possible underlying injustices. Postmodern theorists in particular object to the expansion of state power. One of these was Michel Foucault who wrote *Discipline and punish: the birth of the present* which criticised the idea of punishment and reinterpreted it as a form of state control. Foucault writes about and analyses the experience of the offender throughout history. In his view, punishment is a rational activity designed to maintain power and social control in the hands of the state. Those who hold the reigns of power use punishment in a tactical manner to control the population and so maintain their power and political order. It is not enough simply to have power – it must be wielded.

Foucault's method of deconstruction defines societies in terms of relationships of domination and submission. Because societies are evolving and so ever changing, power continually requires to be enforced by coercion. Since the state has reserved to itself all legitimate use of coercion, it imposes control by means of punishment. Punishment is a demonstration of power – an act of terror. It is also an act of vengeance designed to show the wrath of those with the power against those who do not obey. The reasons of the recalcitrant do not matter.

Punishment is supplemented by lesser correctional regimes. Surveillance increases and all our activities are measured. Rules enter into every aspect of life. Power must expand continually to obliterate all opposition. Failures to adhere to the required standards are corrected: not only by the courts but by all sorts of other means. Economics becomes one of the tools of governmental control. Taxes may be used to correct or discourage forms of behaviour. Correction is a new and gentle form of industrialised punishment. The role of the public is to submit. They must adopt the mind-set of the defeated, of the stupid and unthinking obedient. Shame is an effective means of controlling behaviour at the lowest level. Foucault says that the most effective form of control is a continuing one in which the citizen is continually maintained under submission:

"the ideal point of penality today would be an indefinite discipline: an interrogation without end, an investigation that would be extended without limit to a meticulous and ever more analytical observation, a judgment that would at the same time be the constitution of a file that was never closed, the calculated leniency of a penalty that would be interlaced with the ruthless curiosity of an examination, a procedure that would be at the same time the permanent measure of a gap in relation to an inaccessible norm and the asymptomatic movement that strives to meet in infinity".

Control is all. This is surely a most pessimistic and Machiavellian view.

Essential concepts

- Retributive theories take a simple moral view that the criminal, in committing a crime, has done an evil to the victim which can only be healed by the criminal himself suffering a harm which is equal and opposite in moral seriousness. This involves an essentially backwards look in time to assess the moral evil which the criminal has committed. The punishment should fit the crime.

- The Babylonian King Hammurabi imposed a retributive legal code some 4,000 years ago. Every crime identified was associated with its punishment. Punishments were scaled in accordance to the seriousness of the crime and also the social standing of the criminal and social importance of the harm (for example, crimes against the gods or the King are more serious than those against individual citizens).

- The Biblical *lex talionis* (literally the law of retaliation: "an eye for an eye and a tooth for a tooth, an arm for an arm, a life for a life") is to be found in the Old Testament book of *Leviticus* 24.19–21. In this way satisfaction could be obtained by the victim of the harm and so scores were settled and would not give rise to family feuds.

- Strong retributivists argue that it is enough to punish a deserving criminal with a punishment that fits his crime. Morality is satisfied. Nothing else is required.

- Weak retributivists argue that a criminal must not only deserve to be punished but that the punishment should additionally produce beneficial effects such as deterrence. Moral justification is not enough.

- For both types of retributivism, the punishment must be deserved.

- Utilitarian theories are forward looking and seek the justification for punishment in the ability that a punishment has to produce future good effects and reduce future harms.

- Bentham objected to the excessive nature of some of the punishment regimes imposed in the 18th century. He was concerned that after a crime has been committed it immediately strikes us that to inflict a punishment increases the total amount of pain and suffering in the whole system. The principle aim of punishment is to deter a criminal from future criminal behaviour.

- Other Utilitarian aims involve rehabilitation, therapy and social theories of punishment.

- Rehabilitation is aimed at enabling a criminal to recognise the harm that their criminal behaviour creates and the error of his ways, to learn to avoid forms of criminal behaviour, and learn new forms of behaviour. This may be achieved by the learning of a trade or by other forms of education.

- Therapeutic approaches regard criminal behaviour as an expression of an aberrant character and so they attempt to address the defects in the criminal's character.

- Social theories look at ways of appeasing society for the moral outrage that crimes create. Some social theories give the criminal education and employment training while at the same time campaign for a general improvement in society as a whole.

- Utilitarian theories suffer from some well-known problems. Deterrence may be equally effective where a member of the criminal's family or someone known to him may be punished instead. Therapeutic punishment may result in indefinite sentences.

- Kelsen takes a causal approach to a criminal laws. A law is a norm addressed to the individual citizen and requires him to do or forbear from doing a particular piece of behaviour. But at the same time the law is addressed to an official and obliges him, in the event that the law is breached by the citizen, to impose the relative sanction. The advantages of this approach are two-fold. The purpose of the norm and the importance of the values it protects, are taken seriously, and the citizen is given notice of what will happen to him if he chooses to disobey the norm.

- Foucault criticised the idea of punishment and reinterpreted it as a form of state control. The state uses punishment in a tactical manner to control the population. The effect of this is to assert the state's dominance and force the citizen into submission. As societies are evolving and changing, power continually requires to be enforced by coercion. Surveillance increases, behaviour is measured, rules enter into every aspect of life, opposition must be obliterated. Economics becomes one of the tools of governmental control.

BIBLIOGRAPHY

Aquinas, T, *Summa Theologica*, 10 vols (Forgotten Books, 2007)

Aristotle, *Nicomachean Ethics* (Penguin, 2004)

Austin, J, *The Province of Jurisprudence Determined* (Hackett Publishing, 1998)

——, *Lectures* (Thoemmes Continuum, 2002)

Comte, A, *The Positive Philosophy* (Trübner, 1875)

Durkheim, E, *The Division of Labour in Society* (Palgrave Macmillan, 1984)

Dworkin, R, *Taking Rights Seriously* (Duckworth, 1996)

——, *Law's Empire* (Hart, 1998)

Ehrlich, E, *Fundamental Principles of the Sociology of Law* (Transaction, 2001)

Finnis, J, *Natural Law and Natural Rights* (Oxford Clarendon, 1979)

Foucault, M, *Discipline and Punish* (Penguin, 1991)

Fuller, L, *The Morality of Law* (Yale, 1977)

Grotius, H, *De Jure Belli ac Pacis* (Kessinger, 2009)

Hägerström, A, *Inquiries into the Nature of Law and Morals* (Almvist & Wiksell, 1953)

Hart, H L A, *The Concept of Law* (Oxford Clarendon, 1997)

Hobbes, T, *Leviathan* (Cambridge University Press, 1996)

Hohfeld, W, *Fundamental Legal Conceptions as Applied in Judicial Reasoning* (Lawbook Exchange, 2010)

Hume, D, *A Treatise concerning Human Nature* (Penguin, 2004)

Jhering, R von, *Law as Means to an End* (Lawbook Exchange, 1999)

Kelsen, H, *The Pure Theory of Law* (Oxford University Press, 2007)

Llewellyn, K, *Jurisprudence: Realism in Theory and Practice* (Transaction, 2008)

Locke, J, *Two Treatises on Government* (Cambridge University Press, 1988)
Loevinger, L, *Jurimetrics: the Next Step Forward* (Basic Books, 1963)
Lundstedt, V, *Legal Thinking Revised* (Stockholm, 1956)

MacCormick, D N, *Legal Reasoning and Legal Theory* (Oxford Clarendon, 1994)
—, *Questioning Sovereignty* (Oxford University Press, 1999)
—, *Institutions of Law* (Oxford University Press, 2007)
—, *Practical Reasoning in Law and Morality* (Oxford University Press, 2008)
—, *Rhetoric and the Rule of Law* (Oxford University Press, 2009)
Malinowski, B, *Crime and Custom in Savage Society* (Routledge, 2009)
Marx, K, *Capital: Critique of Political Economy*, 3 vols (Penguin, 2004)
Mill, J S, *On Liberty* (Oxford University Press, 2008)

Nozick, R, *Anarchy, State and Utopia* (Wiley-Blackwell, 2001)

Olivecrona, K, *Law as Fact* (Stevens & Sons, 1971)

Plato, *The Republic* (Penguin, 2007)

Rawls, J, *A Theory of Justice* (Harvard University Press, 1999)
Ross, A, *On Law and Justice* (Lawbook Exchange, 2007)

Savigny, F von, *Vom Beruf unserer Zeit für Gesetzgebung und Rechtswissenschaft* (Nabu, 2010)

Waldron, J, *Theories of Rights* (Oxford University Press, 1985)
Weber, M, *Economy and Society* (University of California, 1992)
Wendell Holmes, O, *The Common Law* (Dover, 1991)

INDEX